IN SITU

Zen at the End of the Row

RALPH THURSTON

authorHOUSE®

AuthorHouse™
1663 Liberty Drive
Bloomington, IN 47403
www.authorhouse.com
Phone: 833-262-8899

Published by AuthorHouse 02/15/2022

ISBN: 978-1-6655-5214-1 (sc)
ISBN: 978-1-6655-5213-4 (e)

Print information available on the last page.

Any people depicted in stock imagery provided by Getty Images are models, and such images are being used for illustrative purposes only. Certain stock imagery © Getty Images.

This book is printed on acid-free paper.

PREFACE

GEORGE CARLIN PERFORMED A COMEDIC
bit about food advertising, the gist being "if it says natural,
it isn't"—after all, you never see broccoli labeled "natural".
Likewise, if it says it's homemade, it isn't. If it "tastes just
like maple syrup" it doesn't. In the spirit of that American
advertising tradition, this book is hardly Zen, though its
title refers to it. The author hasn't been to a monastery,
hasn't sat in meditation, likely possesses not a single Zen
characteristic described in these pages (save by accident),
has just read about it from Zen's outskirts, too lazy to
undertake the practice. But even as a knockoff branding
of the authentic thing, the observations on these pages
may still have merit, being situated not too far inside
Zen to see out, not too far outside to see in. Sharing that
position the reader can hopefully get a bead on what's
being looked at.

Inside, outside. Approaching, leaving. Above,
below. Even the most sedentary of us experiences life
as movement and position, be it others' or one's own,

with every moment bearing the sensation of flowing through a medium or of it flowing right by. This book references a farmer's relationship to that experience, to his work, to his property, and to the world in general, but farming is just one way to be among many. Zen, when adopted, incorporates how we share all those ways, it shadows them, infiltrates them, turns them into a sort of art, really, as Ray Bradbury noted in *Zen and the Art of Writing*, Eugen Herrigel expressed in *Zen and the Art of Archery*, and Robert Pirsig detailed in *Zen and the Art of Motorcycle Maintenance*. Add activities as diverse as samurai swordsmanship, Ikebana flower design, and Japanese tea ceremonies that exemplify Zen attributes, and the question emerges: why leave out flower farming as a Zen receptacle?

Zen appears as one of two stereotypes in popular culture, either as the harsh master striking his meditation-sitting students when they twitch so much as an eye or as the benevolent teacher magically enlightening them. Flower farming stereotypes appear along similar contrasting lines, as either a romantic stroll through a field plucking blossoms and humming show tunes or as a harsh existence of long hours and hard work in the worst of weather conditions. Each stereotype is true, each is false, with their real-life counterparts bouncing between those representations, navigating the physical world but also traversing the meta-world, that place of stereotypes, ideas, concepts, and emotions that refers to the physical. If that wasn't enough of an obstacle course, each person has a "self" that internalizes the patterns he uses for the physical and the meta-worlds, creating yet another layer to negotiate. Zen addresses the confusion of weaving through those obstructions, this book addresses Zen.

The big sell for the Internet Age was how it would unite the world as one. Just as Carlin might have predicted, it does no such thing. Instead, its very nature, coding every bit of visual or auditory information into a series of "0"'s or "1"'s, has filtered through the world as like and dislike, shredding the world into pieces of either/or. Thus, "finding one's tribe" entails identifying the "others", drawing a line between in-group and out-group. Those living in this era and the next thus have yet another obstacle to overcome: to ignore, to assimilate, to put all those pieces back together, Zen being one such way.

You probably know just enough about truffles to know their value in the culinary world, even if you've not tasted them. Zen is like those truffles. You probably understand the difficulty hunting for truffles, how gatherers use pigs or dogs to sniff them out in forests, then dig deep when their animals find them. At a thousand dollars or more a pound those truffles prove quite valuable, but a hunter often comes home without bagging a single one. Zen, as valuable as truffles to many, proves equally elusive, being impossible to recognize if you've no idea what it already is. But once grasped and sampled it almost always develops intrigue, if not addiction. Consider this book the Zen equivalent of a truffle-dog, a guide taking you through the wilderness of being.

Off to the hunt!

IN SITU

IN SITU. LITERALLY, ON SITE. LOCAL. Oncologists describe a cancerous tumor as *in situ* when it remains in its original position rather than metastasizing. In gardening it refers to direct seeding, as opposed to starting elsewhere (and else-when) and then transplanting. *In situ* advises letting a plant self-seed since if it grows somewhere on its own, that place must be where it wants to be. A laissez faire gardener, weary of transplanting failures, is grateful for such a gift and leaves that self-seeded clematis even though it upsets his landscape design. In exchange, he gets a twofold dose of pleasure, the free clematis showered down like manna and a simultaneous infusion of irony: try—and fail, don't try—and prosper, the prodigal son's and his brother's experiences rolled into one.

Counter *in situ* with *ordinis*, "row", from which "order" arises. The row is an early intrusion into nature, perhaps man's first geometrical imposition. Just a line, really, but one that simplifies irrigation, planting, cultivation and

1

harvesting, transforming the gatherer into farmer, no longer a passive recipient of nature's bounty (as well as its wrath) but an assertive, even aggressive, extractor of its possibilities. And no doubt, just an instant behind the first row's arrival came the first argument about its appropriateness. We're still arguing now.

Withness and *againstness*. Two poles of a spectrum between which every farmer operates. Embrace *in situ,* a method of working with nature, and you abandon the row, that perfect symbol of man being aligned against nature—a nature that rarely, if ever, situates anything in a perfectly straight line. Conversely, forget *in situ* and grip the row's linearity, gain use of cultivation tools, irrigation methods, the simplicity of the either/or of weed/flower—and export the effects of your actions into nature, disrupting its cycles, possibly to such a degree that it ceases to provide a willing, able platform for your actions.

Without the row, decision-making proliferates and slows progress, occludes tasks: instead of eliminating all vegetation outside the lines you draw with your planter, you must locate each desired plant, encircle it with attention as you search for intruders that you then destroy; too, you must decide which of the desired gets to live—for almost always, the freely given comes as feast or famine, mats of competing seedlings or their near total absence. Decide to eliminate the row, to quit manipulating the soil, the climate and the species toward its logical extreme and you cease being a farmer. Go ahead, put on the gatherer's hat.

But a gatherer-forager faces the same dilemma the farmer does. What to gather, when to gather it, how much to take and from where—all these questions ask how intrusive mankind should be, ask what is "natural" and what is man's rightful role, how much might be done without disrupting the cycles of nature. Lacking the detailed knowledge of an omniscient mind, both farmer and forager, if concerned at all about the rightness of their actions, must position themselves not just physically amidst nature's beings and objects, but mentally, amidst its processes.

More difficultly, they need to know the acuity of their mental processes that place their actions within nature's—self-awareness comes into play, an internal dialogue questioning, and then either falsifying or verifying, one's assumptions. And while the tracker, cartographer and scientist easily verify their perceptions by cross-checking physical facts with others' findings, the farmer/forager's self-understanding eludes intersubjective confirmation—evident as emotions and sensations seem to those experiencing them, they leave no proof of their existence for others to replicate or verify. There is no peer review. One never really knows whether he is *in situ* or transplanted.

The Zen farmer, the Taoist farmer, even the Jeffersonian yeoman understands positioning in time and space, varying somewhat in philosophies but all leaning toward *withness*, while each modern day commercial farmer wrestles with the same questions from a spot near *againstness*. Any farmer of either ilk shifts himself not just in relation to his crops but in regards to his fellow farmers, to his support systems in market and maintenance, to his customers, and, to a lesser degree, to the world at large. Short of unconscious meandering through nature, all figuratively attach themselves to a row of some sort, however crookedly it may be directed.

The large agribusiness farms, many of them tens of thousands of acres, get stereotyped as being operated by farmers who manipulate their land from a distance much as a puppet master operates a marionette—the bigger the farm the more strings, the longer the strings' reach. Adjust that stereotype slightly by substituting other actors and see the cold eye of the researcher with his project, be it animal to dissect or bacteria to alter, see the surgeon covering his patient's entire body save the small area to be operated on, allowing him to focus on the particular without considering the whole. These stereotypes share a way of looking at the world that gives control and focused understanding.

Smallholders, though they often view the big farmer this way, can view their acreages equally coldly, just as distantly, can consider their acreages as possessions, as projects, things to be handled with adroit cleverness. Though a smallholder uses the large commercial farmer to define exactly what he is not, though he uses a set of tools and methods intentionally *not* those of his dogmatic foe's, nothing prevents him from wielding his technology in exactly the same way, nothing keeps him from treating his acreage much as the large farmer does—in fact, being raised in the same society, he likely receives, accepts and exemplifies the same training and behavior, with only the objects he uses differing, the objectives he moves toward perhaps dissimilar but the process, unbeknownst to him, little changed. He still treats his farm as separate, whether he coddles it with actions of very small increments or whips it into shape with heavy-handed techniques.

Inevitably, overlying his position along the with-against spectrum is how a farmer views himself upon it—his self-awareness or lack thereof. Does he perceive his position accurately or imagine it as being nearer an idealized version of himself? It makes a difference, since any difference between positions on the two spectrums yields chaos, the bridge—if there is indeed a bridge—between them perhaps long and rickety. And beyond his position on the second, mirroring spectrum another important factor comes to play: the character of that perceiving self, its solidity, its flexibility, and the nature of the way it refers, as a thinker, to itself as an actor. Thus, a Zen farmer, being minimally self-reflective, becomes nearly invisible, a faint trail aside a physical being, for at the end of his row just hoed free of weeds, he doesn't turn, pat himself on the back and gloat with the thought "Wow, look what I did!" Nor does he feel the need to record it. Instead, he gets a bump in spirit that this task has been done well. That it *fits*. That he fits the task. He gets an identical boost from someone else completing the same task in the same way.

The Zen farmer's workload, heavy enough being a manual task, is much smaller than his proud cohort's, who carries not only his toil but the weight of the self—a sometimes monumental burden poised against all else, for every instance of self-reflection, self-admonishment, and self-aggrandizement adds another weight, another step to work's natural progression. Those self-attentive moments attach to deeds as do barnacles on ships, spread until they distract from his every task, add an obstacle to each action—conflicting with the Zen tenet of direct perception and making navigation more difficult, his perceptions filled with objects the Zen farmer's lacks.

———

Ah, the stray, pleasant surprise, a gift unasked for and needing no reciprocation. The unexpected bouquet of flowers, seemingly arisen from nothingness and swelling this place and moment to a size greater than those instances surrounding. You have to ask yourself when you receive it: is this how the thief feels, how the bargain-hunter feels; is it how those infatuated with technology feel when they bypass a commonly used method by using a new tool, a novel machine, adding or subtracting a step in a process? As different as taking something is from having it given to you, isn't the giddy feeling sprouting from either somewhat the same? Spill the unnecessary, the unearned, the undeserved into a moment and transform it: a smile when unexpected; a sudden *wink!!* appearing like a Class III rapid; a seedling arising, unplanted—what a gift, what a joy. Unless, of course, it's a weed, its position *in situ*.

Quite an appealing concept, *in situ*, almost akin to magic—until you realize one kochia plant produces thirty thousand seeds and a single wormwood specimen casts three times that, both species self-seeding prolifically but their failures exponentially outnumbering successes. As a botanical strategy, then, *in situ* works well for the species, not so much for the individual.

In situ is a natural experiment, an illustration of the struggle between pessimism and optimism, displaying how each can be simultaneously true and false. Focus on the success and ignore the many failures, focus on the disappointments and miss the success—it all depends on your perspective, whether you're born an individual with traits suited to *in situ* or as one thriving best when coddled, and more importantly, whether you're born to a place and time that fosters prosperity and the luxury of *in situ* sight it affords or instead dropped into an inhospitable environment.

As individuals we should be so lucky as to succeed *in situ,* but evolution scatters us as randomly as a dandelion does its fluff. Hence, almost certainly plunked down into a context ever-shifting, we are always looking for the right place to be, the right thing to do, and the right time to do it, searching for a proper position in time, a correct position in space. Even when we fortuitously discover that place, that time, still a great deal of work remains—we must discern the same for the things around us: what they are, when and where they belong, and our relationship to them. Then, as time progresses, we have to do it again. And again. Such is the nature of change.

In situ faces the same criticism and praise as its close cousin *laissez faire,* an oft-used economics phrase promoting minimal or no government involvement. Letting things be, for those satisfied with the way things are, sounds attractive. For those suffering from the status quo, however, it looks like an excuse to keep them poor and deprived. From the lazy, procrastinating farmer's viewpoint, *in situ* appears as a godsend that alleviates extra work: "See, doing nothing is better than doing something!" while to the fastidious agriculturist it appears to be an excuse to not try harder and do better. Rather than ranking one viewpoint better than another, listing the consequences of each makes more sense: which we choose adopt is subjective and personal, what results from either stance is verifiable and objective.

In situ is not so far, really, from the thief's attitude as he reasons around the normal modes of commerce. "Someone else would have done it if I didn't," a thief might say, just as the mythological Hephaestus said when he tied Prometheus to a mountain to be pecked at by vultures for eternity. *In situ* excuses an individual from moral judgments, "that's just the way it is" his response to actions he knows to be wrong.

Marketers know our larcenous heart when they raise the "free!" banner, have a sale, send out coupons, tell us how much we saved rather than how much we spent— you were there, *in situ*, where the magic happened, grasp your good fortune! Take a stroll through an estate or garage sale and see the opportunistic circling: it's hard to resist the urge to get something for nothing. Talk to a noodling amateur inventor, see how difficult it is for him to squelch the desire to skip a step, how challenged he is to avoid his fascination with any gadget, gimmick, potion or technology that provides a short cut or solves a difficulty—even one heretofore unknown.

But wait a second—aren't all these traits, of the thief's, of the bartering haggler's, of the technologically enthralled, a way to alter or move oneself, one's desire, one's project away from the way things are, thus directly opposed to *in situ*? Yes, and herein lies the conundrum: defining what is natural in the world, defining your natural state, defining the natural positioning of the two. Sans consciousness, moving with the natural flow of existence may be easy, but with awareness comes judgment and with judgment comes doubt.

The notion of *in situ* refers to letting nature take its course. It speaks as an alternative to forcefully intruding into that flow. But what entails interference? How much intrusion affects nature beyond repair? When, if ever, should a technique or tool be used? More importantly, what is "nature", what is "mankind" and what relationship between the two is proper? How much of nature's resources does mankind rightfully get? Lacking the technology to do much damage, for a long time farmers acted as they wished and rarely faced such questions, but in this era of abundance and its consequent luxury of time to investigate and judge, everything a farmer does gets probed.

You know the words. Natural. Organic. Sustainable. Regenerative. Permaculture. There will be more words to follow in the future, the realm of talk being as vulnerable as fashion to trend changes. In the spirit of keeping-up-with-the-Joneses, a farmer must be aware of these latest terms and their underlying philosophies, methods and attendant gadgets. But an impish theoretical twist accompanies the Jones race in that, aiming for less interference with the soil and less impact on nature, keeping-up really means staying-behind—in the persistent argument regarding the role of *ordinis*, less is always more, a race toward zero impact and a finish line of complete non-involvement.

The irony continues, as the stripping away of man's footprint seems to entail the proliferation, not the dissipation, of his primary trace: technique. Much as the Buddhist acolyte community becomes more self-oriented than the uninitiated everyday Joe on the way to no-self, the back-to-nature farmer grows ever fond of technique and manipulation, those very things that resulted in ecological destruction. Hyperconscious of both new and old instruments and methods, he seeks to become more adept than the commercial farmer at tweaking the world. He may think of himself as an artist.

Few work more closely with nature than farmers, though large agriculturists ironically call each other "windshield farmers", locked in as they are to the farm radio, the cell phone, the desk, the meetings with fieldmen, advisors and bankers. They may hit a hundred thousand miles a year driving from acreage to parts house to bank to fertilizer company to field. Naturalists and those in biological sciences spend a lot of time around nature, too, observing and often experimenting, but their actions almost always entail a separation between nature as an observed object and themselves as the observing, acting subject. Nature is their project, sometimes their playground, like a canvas is for the artist, the blank page is for the writer, the test tube is for the scientist. Farmers interacting with the natural world, on the other hand, find themselves inside the juggling act of biological organisms, tossed about by weather, insect, fungus, and bacteria, and though some consider nature as something to be manipulated—remember the biblical injunction to "subdue the earth"?—, others take a more Zenlike or Taoist stance of partnership with, or even submission to, nature. They are inside the canvas, on the page, in the test tube, interacting with the contents therein and thereon, not observing them, however distantly, as something separate. From such a position, though accurate judgment looms almost impossible, some sort of attitude and appraisal must be adopted to maintain existence: there has to be a way to determine one's place and direction, a way to distinguish being given something rather than taking it.

———

People unacquainted with farmers often use them as examples of eternal optimism—who else would plant every year despite crop failures, weather disasters and market busts? But farmers describe themselves more complexly, typically repeating a wry joke that, to them, never gets old: a reporter asks the farmer who has just won the lottery what he's going to do with his winnings, and after considerable pondering the farmer replies, "I guess I'll just keep farming until it's all gone."

That first walk through the field in the spring, the lupine's leaves emerging like hands in prayer, the peony's tapered, burgundy fingernails reaching upwards, too, and the delphinium's first appearance with its celery-like leaves, lend metaphor to optimism, life triumphant after winter's long imposed dormancy. And each time a species first comes to bloom, that too lifts all but the most hardened spirit, is always a surprise even when expected and always whispers of promise. Later in the season, there are other sensory notes newly provided: bend close to a bunch of lupine and inhale, gather the strong smell of pepper, its ill-fittingness gifting a minor glee; smell the grape Kool-Aid scent that snapdragons unexpectedly exude; or be overwhelmed by the blast from the fans of a greenhouse full of sweet peas, the day's heat progressing and bringing forth aromas intended to entice. And enjoy, too, even the unpleasant scents of candytuft, of rowan, of crambe, of silver lace vine, as they move into the "switch" phase of bait-and-switch, their initial pleasant fragrances, evolved to lure pollinators, giving way to sour resentment and the tiredness of a spent relationship.

But then there is the hailstorm. The root disease that drops larkspur in a single day. The mildew spreading from the delphinium to the *Rudbeckia*, then further through the field, to the peonies, the *Physocarpos*, the calendula.

The aphid outbreak on the snapdragons, their white casings as minuscule as ash randomly scattered across the leaves, later becoming more obvious as tiny splashes with a shiny glint, that exudation turning greasy and black as populations explode and move to the sunflowers, to the cerinthe, and even to the rarely afflicted, the Queen Anne's lace, the cosmos, the grasses. How about the spider mites overwhelming the dahlias, sneakily starting at ground level and working upwards so swiftly that their speed seems incalculable; the same pests smothering the cockscomb celosia heads with their webbing, dulling the *Asclepias tuberosa* and *Asclepias curassavica* leaves and blooms, marring the *Nigella Transformer* pods, infesting the Green Mist *Ammi majus*, ruining the *Cosmos sulphureous*. And the voles, tunneling under winter snow cover through what must be very tasty scabiosa, devouring its roots and then gnawing the nearby drip tape as another exhibit of animal vandalism. The list goes on. And on.

An optimist, the adage goes, ignores reality, while a pessimist ignores possibility. A realist stands above and outside the contest between the two, aware of both the likely and unlikely. The Zen farmer positions himself similarly—*in situ*, you might say, meeting the acreage where he's been placed with what he's been given, ignoring any external or internal chatter assessing his place in time and space. You might call a no-till farmer Zen, right up to the point where he becomes a tinker obsessed with tools, to when he becomes manic for constant improvement or fixed upon being more clever than both nature and his cohorts. But you might call an agribusinessman Zen, too, if he uses his tools wisely and only when necessary, if he treats his customers and employees respectfully, if he defers to his milieu as bigger than him and sets himself humbly amidst it. Whether Zen or not-Zen, it's more a matter of positioning, of your relationship to what surrounds you, and less a matter of where you find yourself positioned.

Once the farmer gets a feel for his context—is he amid moving objects (i.e., mental constructs) or relatively stationary ones—he assesses his situation and acts accordingly. To determine more closely a proper *situatedness* he might be served well to use a model, the computer program Craig Reynolds developed to simulate flocking behavior—a tool appropriate for humans since we are each always one bird amongst a mob of many, one object amidst a plethora of others necessarily avoided.

Reynolds created objects on a screen he called *boids* and programmed three simple rules into each: it should try to maintain a minimum distance from other objects and *boids*, match velocity with neighboring *boids*, and move toward the perceived center of the mass of *boids* nearby. With just these three directives *boids* created murmurations and avoided crashing into each other or hitting obstacles on the computer screen. Let's call such flocking an example of Zenlike behavior, and a seamless flight without collisions a source of not just minor pleasure but a sense of movement and belonging to a greater flow than just the self.

Compare the *boids'* flocking model to the hierarchical behaviors more customary to the lives we're born to and more akin to the way we're taught to think. Consider, possibly, the structure geese use, flying not in the shimmering, murmurating form starlings exhibit but in a V-shape, an apex bird leading the two slanted legs of the flock. Since, unlike in most hierarchies, individual geese of the flock take turns leading—a democratic, rather than autocratic, structure—maybe ponder instead the more authoritarian wolf pack, an alpha male leading the group until a younger, stronger specimen challenges and usurps his position. Or look at the primates that form dominance hierarchies. Closer yet to home, those junior high student experiences so like the pecking order exhibited in a chicken coop.

Farmers, highly specialized primates, tend to transpose their experience of the hierarchies witnessed in church, in school, in government, in family, onto the things of the world that lack them. That viewpoint serves as a tool, a template to order the world, one useful until applied where inappropriate—as in assessing those trends both local and global that erupt without single leaders or instigating events. Look to the playground or a county fair, where mobs spontaneously arise, sometimes frighteningly so, out of one's control and wholly lacking a plan, to see an alternate structure that grows more organically, plantlike from the ground up, rather than starting from an idea dispersed from above and following a guided, preconceived path downward.

Few of us resist hiding moblike, random chaos with an explanation fitting the hierarchical notions we're accustomed to. In a structured societal milieu we possess a position, and as unpleasant as it might be we find it less so than being amidst a mob. When we assess others as above and others as below and yet others as semi-equals, to the side of us, we find our place, be it as boid or goose, whereas lacking any framework to determine others' positions we flail about, unable to discern our own. The *boids'* template gives us an explanation of complex behavior, sifts out order from chaos and offers us a feel for a sort of movement not driven by anxiety, a sensation perhaps like riding a surfboard or skiing.

But let the flock land. Thus bound to the earth, use a more stable, stationary model to assess position, one with a broader, more distant view like the Serenity Prayer, a fixture of Alcoholics Anonymous which all of us, including the farmer, should find useful: God grant me the serenity to accept the things I can't change, the courage to change the things I can, and the wisdom to know the difference. In succinct shorthand it offers a way to order the universe, a method to find our place. You may remember Venn diagrams from an early math class—circles of sets, some overlapping—and see how, by using the Serenity Prayer, you might draw a small circle of those things within your locality that you can change, then draw a larger circle that surrounds it that includes other sets of things you normally might attend to but lack power to affect. Framing existence this way, the world becomes more manageable—and in a way that disperses anxiety and eliminates the need to stop the always-in-motion collection of object we call nature. Optimism dissipates along with pessimism, leaving the bare, clear facts of existence through which to move.

———————

To navigate through the actual world, our brains devote cells to both self-centered (egocentric) and other-centered (allocentric) positioning, both types being required for effective travel and movement—we need to know where other things are, where we are, and then develop the relationship between those positions. Hence, border cells define walls, fencelines, and hedges, place cells refer to personal locations we have been, and grid cells situate objects in relation to one another. The size of the grid varies, much like a map, so can be a room or a desert, can comprise an entire ocean, the spatial ratios between the objects within differing accordingly. Its flock might be in each *boid's* mental grid, a farmer's property in his.

A common image of farmers has two (in overalls, of course) meeting on opposite sides of a fenceline, tonguing succulent, green wheat stems at the corners of their mouths. The character of their relationship flows from their talk: weather, markets, gossip about other farmers. Occasionally, they agree on a subject, but mostly the discussion is a sort of verbal fencing—the idiom "feeling each other out" describes their activity. If they have a great deal in common, one might echo the other, and if they exchange work from time to time their conversation may enter into a comfortable volley that aims for and reaches a profitable end. But farmers of differently sized acreages, while seemingly agreeing, often talk past one another, their mental grids sized according to experience: the words and concepts they use, while meaning the same to each of them, are applied to maps bearing little resemblance. Think of the Texas rancher who lets a smallholder ride with him in his pickup: "I can drive and drive and drive all day and never get from one side of my spread to the other," he brags, his rider nodding knowingly and replying, "Yeah, I had a pickup like that once."

The backyard gardener's success isn't the thousand-acre farmer's; the designer's "all your sunflowers", pictured as coming from a small garden plot, isn't the two thousand stems coming to bloom weekly on a two acre farm.

While scientists have not found a grid conforming to such mismatching definitions, it doesn't require much insight to apply the brain grid/border/place cell model to plot how confusion arises when one mind situates terms differently than another. The terms, though the same, reside in different contexts with different spatial relationships between them.

You no doubt noticed mice or rats running along barn walls, maybe witnessed humans similarly holding to tree lines, to sidewalks or fences. Cattle tend to pace fencelines (as do some farmers), particularly when newly pastured, and most animals shy from open spaces when alone—watch a pheasant scurry through an open field and witness full distress. Border cells give reference points, and are both egocentric and allocentric. But place cells always refer to the self, fire when I near somewhere I have been and providing memory for my return—déjà vu, you might conjecture, is a misfire of such cells. Grid cells, while representing the outside world, do so from a personalized point of view. We navigate physicality using these cells and likely, in similar fashion, guide our paths similarly through the meta-worlds we create.

Scientists are just now refining neurological discoveries of how we navigate, how we mark locations, objects and our position amidst them, but they'll be working far longer on how we make our way through private, conceptual representations. It goes without saying, though, that even if concepts and emotions have no set of brain cells corresponding to them as do the features of the physical world, we nonetheless borrow those representations when we say "don't go there" or "his head's in the clouds", when we claim to be "under the weather" or "over the moon". Without those corresponding notions we wouldn't think "outside the box" or be "in a rut", and no act would be "beneath us", no desired object would be "out of our league". Likewise, we remember past moments when we *approach* modestly similar events (the equivalent of place cells firing?), sometimes disturbingly so, making us *retreat*. And our mental and sensory grids vary in size from all-encompassing (religious beliefs and philosophical concepts) to minuscule (the finely-sliced aesthetic or sensual sensation). We can't verify such mental and emotional navigation as we do physical wayfaring, but we nonetheless make our way through some sort of place, however fumblingly.

The grid cell setup in the brain provides a way to explain the differences in worldviews of an extremely rural farmer, whose acreage might span many, many miles with houses sparsely appearing and other differences virtually absent, and a suburban or urban farmer with neighbors right next door, traffic regularly passing, noise relatively constant and empty space nigh nonexistent. Each uses his grid to navigate within it. But if you grow up in the tightly spaced inner city, then get transported into the

Alaskan tundra, or if you grow up in rural Nebraska, then find yourself in New York City's canyons, you'll experience how different your situatedness is from the local inhabitants'. Conifers' needles can't respond to temperature changes of too great a range so consequently explode, and you may do the same, your grid set up for one existence creating unmanageable dissonance when placed in another one.

———

My idea of a good time
Is walking my property line
And knowing the mud on my boots is mine…

So sings the Marshall Tucker Band, expressing the landowner's pride and the renter's wish. Territoriality strikes man's heart just as it does the robin's and the bear's, we've just created agreements to eliminate renegotiation every morning.

Beyond the legal and financial morass that underpins that property line, beyond the cultural and philosophical foundations that brought us to first imagine it and to then accept it, lies a hidden, unconscious wealth of meaning, a set of attitudes and beliefs specific to the individual, unlike the accompanying surveyor's stakes that delineate a particular place that law-abiders agree upon.

One's property is a nexus, as is any physical or temporal point in the universe. To some it means "not yours", to others it means "mine", the two outlooks at first glance seeming the same. But the "not yours" camp has an eye on outsiders and the "mine" has its back to them, their resultant realities sharing little beyond an acceptance of property lines. If my attention focuses on others, my life and the way I live it differs from the way I live if I attend to myself and, by extension, the world inside my property line. A different set of things lie behind me, stand outside my attention, and as a consequence I am a different person.

For some, property is not just an expression of self but its extension. *Having* property is thus *being* property. Trespassing equates to insult. For others, property—a farm, for instance—assumes the status of a project. And for yet another set of individuals, an area defines a place to be in and to move through, almost a fabric upon which their lives perform a sort of three-dimensional needlepoint.

Any project reveals the nature of its steward, its manipulator, its handler. One dog trainer uses punishment as a means to mold his subject, another focuses on reward and teaching. One farmer considers his spread as a living, a means to an end, another relates to it as a responsibility, and yet another considers it as a dance partner of sorts, the two of them conducting a physical and temporal dialogue.

Their methods tell of the ways they interpret the world and consequently the way they must act.

The way a farmer thinks about his property informs his methods: go forth and subdue the earth, the Bible says, excusing one way of being, its opposing method of living *with* nature embodied in Lao Tse's *Tao Te Ching*. But if you used a farmer's bookshelf to predict how his farm looked or how he farmed you'd probably be less accurate than had you cast a set of dice. Only when you witnessed the farm itself could you infer his true, rather than expressed, beliefs.

The end of the row is one place to draw such inferences. Inferences of many sorts. It's a telling place. Most any worker, newbie or veteran, tends to relax his standards here. A statistician, one unacquainted with agriculture, might be astonished to see his bell curve illustrated so perfectly in the physical world: the row's tail end and its head serving as the curve's outlying cusps and thus unrepresentative of the general; the beginning possibly over-diligent, the end likely hurriedly and sloppily done. But those tails speak of character, the traits of the weeder, the planter, the sprayer, and the harvester. They measure his thoroughness, how strictly he adheres to habits and beliefs, how swiftly he loses attention, how eager he is to be done.

The facts at the row's end nakedly display the worker's acts, but there, at the row's end, a more difficultly measured essence erupts in the way the worker experiences a task completed. Does he "own" his labor as he owns his property—is he proud of a job well done, somewhat ashamed of a poor performance? Or does he look back to see a scene of activity, an aesthetic sprawl not tied to himself but rather an intrinsic expression? Or, does he not look back at all, but go to the next row without pause to continue working? And, if he doesn't pause for even a short appraisal, does he begin the next row in a foul mood, his work a weight he wished he were done with, or does he make the turn joyously, lost in the unfolding task?

To have a farm, to hoe a row, to those raised in a typically Judeo-Christian milieu, is to acquire a sort of self-capital, a measure of worth much like money, and just as possessing property extends one's reach, accomplishment expands the self. But there are other ways to consider having and doing—those immersed in Eastern traditions like Zen or Taoism eliminate the self as a reservoir to be filled with either material acquisitions or egotistical accomplishments. If the West can be reduced to a rat race of keeping-up-with-the-Joneses, the East might be distilled into its opposite, staying-behind-the-Smiths—with one exception: there is, for the Eastern purist, no competition with others, just a continuing effort to be rid of the thing that reflects, at the end of the row or at the property line, upon itself.

Call current times the selfie era, an historical period that elevates all moments, stores them, talks about them, then talks about the talk talking about them (as is being done here, on this page). In a sense, this self-centeredness always existed but now accelerates, much as bodily understanding rapidly expanded when scientists began dissecting cadavers: though there was always the human body, peeling it open revealed a new way of understanding it; likewise there was always an internal dialogue of consciousness but one that is now audibly and visibly dissected and documented, in finer and finer increments, via the computer age. We spend more time looking back at the end of the row, it sometimes seems, than time on it.

When weeding, almost everyone relaxes his standards at the end of the row. Nigh perfect at the task through the rest of the row, something about the end changes the process. Some may say "good enough", "C" work being sufficient from their point of view; some may rush, glad to be done, though a dozen or a hundred like rows remain; some may just lose focus, their minds taking in the empty perimeter and throwing off their concentration. The strange change at the row's end may even be nature's inherent way of introducing novelty—maybe we're programmed toward imperfection, to allow that five percent at the bell curve's tails to usher in difference, mutation, diversity.

In any case, the row's end turns out to be a bad place to let down one's guard since it's often the entry point for both botanical and insect intruders. But it's a good place for chaos to insert itself. Any point of change proves so, it turns out, with every line we draw, every wall we erect, intending to introduce order but inadvertently serving as the place for newness to arise. Look at the fence at the property line, weeds collecting, cattle hair on the barbs, gopher mounds along its path, bird droppings on its wires and posts, snowdrifts lining it in winter, a host of insects lurking at it ready to populate the field.

But we need that property line. Just as a scientist needs to define the parameters of his experiment, the farmer requires finitude lest his tasks flow out like water from a broken container. We need the self that is looking back on the row, too, as a similar construction: without the parameters we call *self*, imagined though they might be, we just sprawl across the vast landscape of consciousness.

Zen aims for just such a thing, an end to parameters, the extinction of the self, and as individuals we seek that end, almost universally, though through different modes of being: religious ecstasy, drug induced stupor, romantic love, even fascism annihilates the confines of self, and all provide succor just as all end badly. Farmers often wish to escape, too, from the farm they artificially divided from the rest of reality. Their dream, initially a thing drawing them forward into harvest's promise, instead morphs, toward the last days of summer, into the acid trip that just won't end.

The self is a tricky beast, and property as its extension proves equally tricky. Do we own our farm or does it own us—it might be asked about any project, and is illustrated most concisely with Thomas Jefferson's description of slavery: "we have the wolf by the ear, and we can neither hold him nor safely let him go." It's a relationship that the lesser-involved spouse often complains about, maybe wishing the couple lived away from the farm so it wasn't always beckoning at the door like the high tide surf from the beach.

You can visualize yourself as a shaper of the universe, a God outside his project or even a researcher outside his rat maze or centrifuge. If the farmer sees his relationship with the farm as such, it necessarily becomes other than him. Or he can perceive himself as inside the farm, a part of it, sometimes submitting and other times dominating— and occasionally sharing its authority.

If a shaper, you consider yourself in control, as needing to control. You whip the farm into shape like a dog trainer unafraid to use a shock collar. If you take the Zen mode of action, you more likely farm within a set of perceived parameters—you nudge your plants, go easy on the soil. But these are imagined stereotypes, fairy tales of sorts, ends of an agriculture spectrum—the demonized commercial farmer with chemicals, genetically modified seeds, oversized acreages and equipment on one end, the magician/alchemist/shaman farmer on the other, incorporating a set of nature's instructions that, if properly understood, somehow evades fungal and insect pest, foul weather, and weed infestation. Few farmers fit either description though most subscribe to one or the other. You might liken the dichotomy to H.L. Mencken's characterization of man as either worshipping a past Golden Age or a utopian future. Both tendencies harken toward stasis, both drain the present and its many possibilities by focusing on an imaginary endpoint.

The Serenity Prayer, AA members' shorthand directive for prioritizing the world, proves effective for all of us. The farmer should know his climate, for instance, but he should know he can't change it—he can tweak, with the aid of technology, aspects of his climate using man made structures, planting windbreaks, lengthening days with an artificial light source, tempering excess heat with a cooling system, avoiding excess cold with an array of heaters, adding shade in overly light areas, and using fans to create air flow, but he cannot alter the climate. He can change the way he treats his plants, but he can't alter their genetic proclivities—each species has its parameters beyond which it will not grow, among them a soil PH level tolerance, a temperature range (tropical plants won't survive frost, alpine plants don't usually like heat), water needs (succulents need very little, aquatic plants need a lot), and sun/shade requirements. They have different habits regarding blooming, some triggered by daylength, some by heat, some perennials needing vernalization and others not, with some species refusing alteration and others forgiving—they'll bloom anytime, given the right ingredients. Some have different habits after harvesting, many continuing to open if cut in the bud and others, like zinnias and butterfly weed, halting that operation immediately. Neither climate nor the species' parameters can be changed but they can be understood. Must be understood, in fact, for a successful farm.

What can the farmer change? His irrigation schedule, his timing, his demeanor when dealing with customers, his quality levels, quantity levels—and all these things are dependent on things he has either no control over (the climate) or somewhat little control over (his markets). Knowing the difference between what he can tweak and what he can't, that's where his wisdom comes in.

But back to the end of the row, where the fastidious planter, faced with an empty space and no seeds or transplants to fill it, decides to widen the spaces between plants already planted in the row's interior so the row ends look even. Where the hoer who hates his job, or perhaps just suffers from boredom, speeds his efforts in the interest of being finished, his attention deteriorating. Where the worker competing for points, in a system in which an omnipresent being he imagines keeps score, looks back and smugly says, "I did that," his pride bursting at the seams. Or, where the monk looks back, appreciates the work and says, if saying anything, "That is done," without reference to self.

Farmers often scout the ends of rows for a quick sampling of insect infestation. Host plants in nearby untended areas cast overpopulating species to the closest alternatives, those at the end of row. Row ends, subject to the elements of weather even as they protect interior neighbors, show stress first—a lack of water, too much water (if near low lying areas), wind damage.

The Greek term *hesuchia*, though referring to the moment of rest after the *agon*, the contest, might apply to the end of row, one thing finished, that thing referenced in a moment of perusal. You might stretch Alfred North Whitehead's notion of the *occasion*, the smallest drop of subjective experience, to describe that place in time, that end of the row, too—Whitehead considered the self to be a string connecting such "rows", the components of completed moments the fodder for the current one, the current one a resource for the next. One row finished, another occasion coming up. Gregory Bateson, riffing on Whitehead, would call the end of the row an occasion and the witnessing of one's work a meta-occasion, a thing-about-the-thing.

The way we tie up an occasion, the way we appraise what we do—what happens at the end of the row, that place of not just difference but (in Batesonian terms) a *difference-that-makes-a-difference*, might be a small sample of experience from which to draw conclusions about our character, about the way we know and the way we act, but of the pool of small samples it might be the best and most accurate. How focused are we, how distracted? How do we treat the task, and by extrapolation the world in general? Perhaps most importantly, how do we perceive our relationship to the row? Must "that mud on my boots (be) mine", does it have value only in relation to us, do we need an "objective" judgment to derive pleasure, to generate impetus?

A farmer, or a farmworker, who perceives himself as *inside* his farm acts differently than one perceiving himself as *outside* and separate from it. He experiences his work, the world and himself differently, alters his actions accordingly. Inside the farm, as if, perhaps, in a snow globe, his attention turns outward, to the sky; outside the farm, as if holding the snow globe in his hand, he looks downward at the object he holds. His project. The farm. The two perspectives differ immensely, the two farmers walking their property lines as if members of different species.

———

Potato farmers have, at least since the advent of the four-row planter, referred to the place where one set of rows abuts the next as the "guess row". At harvest time a narrow guess row results in cut potatoes ruined by either the digger blade or vine-splitting coulter, while a wide row wastes space, creating a place for weeds to evade cultivation or chemicals. GPS eliminates those problems today, but in the past a tractor driver could earn mythic status by making straight passes with guess rows not easily discerned, particularly on sloping hillsides that tempted slippage. Think of the place where the self abuts earlier action as a guess row with like results, with the driver who looks back to survey his labor losing track of his path forward, his steering hand drifting in the same direction that he twists to eye his work, throwing his pass awry and spreading or narrowing the guess row.

Hillsides and swales, where gravity works against the driver's intention, inspire flaws, as do the ends of the rows. There, the driver might begin the pass prematurely and awry without fully squaring the tractor, or he might end the pass with a too early twist of the steering wheel, impatient to return in the opposite direction. Any such curve at the end, if not immediately corrected on the next pass, increases its length, width and resultant convexity or concavity, one swath at a time, each new set of rows exacerbating the collective mistakes of those prior.

Even more likely to cause a crooked or bad guess row, the sway of a tractor's draft arms have to be taken into account—how much play do they have, are they slightly akilter, is one higher than the other? A source of more mistakes: parallax, the nature of vision itself, having two eyes with separate lines of sight meeting at a single object, giving us the sense of three-dimensionality. While the tractor is in motion, the object of the driver's parallax vision constantly changes, each time it does so opening the door for mistakes. Focus on your finger held in front of your eyes, see one, then focus beyond it but keep your eyes in the same place and see two. That cross-eyed doubleness fades in an out for the driver just as it does for any self-reflective being looking back, then looking ahead, then looking at the present.

The guess row, then, is a place where mistakes accumulate, where the intention at one pass abuts the intention of the next—and to some extent fails to do so. Most of us having multiple intentions, we're bound to end up with problems at the guess row, where our aims conflict, often unconsciously. We wish to make a task easy, for instance, but don't want to use technology that depletes resources. We wish to make a profit, but shy from methods that enable that to happen. We wish to properly take care of our farm, but want to take a vacation when the farm needs us most. We want to get a crop planted, but don't want to face the elements. Oftentimes, we're well aware of the apples-and-oranges nature of these choices, but likely as often we can't see their incompatibility, may even deny it. The Zen farmer, aware of the different threads of experience that create the braid-like nature of existence, eliminates denial from his repertoire of tools and loses no time or energy choosing or assessing his choice.

———

Like no-till agriculture, Zen's aim for no-mind and no-self echoes Lao-Tse's instruction to govern a great nation "as you would cook a small fish." That philosophy of wielding a light touch presumes a universe that, if not overly meddled with, ultimately unfolds in an orderly, even benevolent manner, and it considers man's natural state as fitting its social environment snugly, not painfully—a concept not so far removed from Rousseau's "noble savage", a forerunner of much back-to-earthism. On the farm, it implies using the least invasive methods possible, keeping mechanical tilling to a minimum, returning matter to the soil, restraint when using chemical or mineral amendments—basically, eliminating human interference. It implies a farmer should possess poise, aplomb, *je ne sais quoi,* a knowledge of an acreage and its inhabitants and moreso, a willingness to be a part of them, even subservient to them—the farmer should, basically, erase himself.

What is tillage if not self-reference, a churning in of the soil upon itself—the same sort of activity Zen discipline seeks to evade. But even without a farmer's intrusions, soil rotates its particles through erosion, through frost and thaw, with the activity of microbes and insects, with the more aggressive actions of animals like earthworms and burrowing rodents—tillage just greatly speeds up that natural process. Consider the Zen self as having a similarly recursive, cyclical character that stays streamlined when operating at a natural speed, one without the extraordinary array of mental tools we've created: denial, excessive rumination, obsession, deflection and unwarranted attention—each the psychical equivalent of rotovator tines. The Zen farmer sets down those habits and tools, instead holds close to a minimalist self, creating no myth, needing no story.

And what is a farmer if not an instrument of change, someone who fiddles with nature, speeding it up or directing its path elsewhere—even if ever-so-slightly, as Zen instructs? What is a human if not a self—an entity aware of itself? Remove the farmer's actions and ultimately no farm exists, remove the self, its pride and peccadilloes, and what unenvisionable being remains? It's difficult to think of such resultant nothingness, though many philosophers have tried to do just that.

No-mind and no-till inevitably lead to this same box canyon: zero impact, erasure, pulling one piece at a time from the Jenga tower of self or farm until it topples and disappears. But most Buddhists and most farmers put on the brakes as they near the logical conclusions of their philosophical premises, much like St. Augustine did as he prayed for God to save him from his sinful ways—but to not do so just yet. So, just as the end of the row gets sloppily weeded, their philosophies get a little frayed as they near their logical ends.

That row's end conundrum is not a new problem. Theravada, the original Buddhism, reached it when its aim of self-annihilation in the form of *nirvana* (enlightenment) became too difficult or unpalatable, a dead-end to most, inspiring the Mahayana offshoot that, while adhering to nirvana as a goal, puts it on the back burner. How? By hedging its teachings and insisting that the enlightened, rather than being transported from the birth-and-death of life, return to the everyday as *bodhisattvas* to assist the rest of humanity toward the same state. Much later in the West, Protestantism sprang from Catholicism in a similar row's-end manner to focus on working in, rather than transcending, the world. Good works, not sainthood or martyrdom, were the new goal.

Today's green movement wrestles with a similar problem, its noble goals, when taken to their logical end, ultimately resting on man's disappearance. The eco-friendly, fumbling for a way out of dogmatic self-annihilation, search for their own Protestantism, their own Mayahana Buddhism, a way to tweak their self-destructive row's-end logic to give mankind a sliver of space in the world before they end up like the Shakers, whose renunciation of procreation took its adherent population into a death spiral that rendered it extinct.

Many green adherents grasp at new technology for a magic fix, unable (or unwilling) to fathom that the desire for the magic fix, the fetishization of technology, ushered in the problem they wish to solve. A separate strain of environmentalism reaches backwards, rather than forward, to save the world, resurrecting lost traditions while neglecting to consider that ancient methods may be lost for good reason, through attrition caused by accumulated failures and not through conspiratorial action. Most of the ecologically minded, though, accustomed to the habits of shopping, take some products from category A (utopia) and some from category B (the Golden Age of the past) to create a random mishmash with predictable results and of peculiar character. There tack seems to emulate parallax, two separate visions merging at a single point, making sense at the moment but only then, and beyond and before it yielding a blurred doubleness. Never before have the two separate urges, one oriented towards utopia and one toward an Edenic past, been so recurrently intertwined, the futuristic and the quaint fused so tightly into a cobbled-up existence.

How unlike Zen.

Most of us don't aspire to no-self, we just want a more manageable self. We want a lean farm, not a no-farm.

One that, while disturbing the cosmos somewhat, does so as lightly as possible. We want our place in space and time without exceeding our rightful territories. Purists disdain such a view as wishy-washy and hypocritical but nature shares it, always leaving wiggle room as a way to usher in change. Nature erupts with mutations, is filled with parasites and decay. It sports the predator-prey relationship, beautiful only to those uninvolved. All these things, perhaps perfect in their own way, provide a way out of perfection, that dead end that leads to stasis and permanence.

We see at the end of almost any row, whether it be weeded by the lazy, the amateur, or the experienced, how perfection drifts toward imperfection. Just like any edge or boundary, be it beach or epidermal layer, the row's end blurs distinctions. It's where change occurs. The weeder, seeing the field's border, lets his guard down. The road or the aisle distracts him, the thought of being finished hurries him, his doggedness slips, his standards shift, and he leaves a few weed seedlings he otherwise wouldn't. Considering the omnipresence of the tendency, you might think it to be instinctive.

It may very well be. The weeder leaves a few weeds much as a forest fire leaves an unburned copse here and there, much as a bear leaves a few berries, much as your friends leave that last piece of pizza. Both Eastern and Western thought possess models to explain this, the Taoist

Yin-Yang symbol and the statistical Bell Curve looking at the occurrence in their own distinct fashions. The Yin-Yang, a circle sliced in half by an "S", one side black and one white, the black side with a white eye, the white side with a black one, represents how opposites not only abut but are part of a single thing, with the eyes representing the opposite-within-its-opposite that everything holds. Let's call this eye *allos,* the Greek word for "other".

Allos appears in Western statistics as the cusps of a Bell Curve, those tails that represent the outliers of any sample. A shotgun blast on a wall visually explains a Bell Curve, most of the bb's distributed in the center—which the hump of the curve models—and a few landing further away (the curve's tails). For metaphor's sake, let's just say there's a mental trigger in all of us that insists we cut a little slack in everything we do, that we shoot a few bb's awry. Only with dedicated practice do we overcome this tendency, and only in life arenas (like rocket science, not like farming) that require extreme precision do we need to.

We honor *allos* when we leave a sacrifice, when we tithe, when we take a day of rest. We use the principle of *allos* when we aesthetically judge and when we learn. *Allos* is the improbable but possible, residing in those Bell Curve tails, and from our earliest learning as a child we separate the unlikely and the unwanted into the category of *allos.* Hence, as we learn and age our world shrinks, for we shave that end of the row off at Instance One, shave another piece of that shrunken row at Instance Two—on and on, in the act of judging, making the universe smaller, the row shorter. When young people dismiss their elders' wisdom they do so instinctively, recognizing the diminishment of possibilities inherent in the aging and learning process. Such dismissal, paradoxically enough, illustrates the process, too: eliminating in one wide brushstroke the potential held in the words of the experienced. And that's how the world regenerates, Yin begetting Yang begetting Yin.

Non-mainstream farmers roll out the learning process almost continually, trying new species, attempting to extend seasons, coddling barely hardy species, and facing the prospect of selling them in changing market climates. If only markets were zoned like climates, they might wistfully imagine, for a flower selling well during one era goes dark in another, another easily marketed in one locale finds disfavor elsewhere. Though trends repeat, any farmer's lifespan or career may not encompass two eras of similar likes that occur possibly decades apart. Hence, if a woody perennial fails to sell when it comes to bloom for him he may tear it out—then regret the action four years later when clients clamor for it. Or, he may test an annual and find it in great demand from one or two sought-after clients, triple his planting and sell no product at all in following seasons. His time frame being shorter than the design cycle, he makes premature but necessary decisions regarding future plantings, their rightness or wrongness impossible to determine beforehand.

A new grower, witnessing these acquired prejudices and the foreshortened old-timer's universe, makes a quick, if premature, judgment: being of another time, the old-timer's impressions and experiences lack immediate value. Missing in that viewpoint is his temporal proximity to the past generations and those following—though he may recognize the *boids* in his flock, know his position on his mental grid, he is blind to a corresponding, intersecting grid that intersects generationally. He is close to those coming before him, close to those who follow, yet he perceives them as almost infinitely distant. Ever so close to a Zenlike flow in one sense but fully apart in another, he repeats mistakes his predecessors made—intentionally, perhaps, hoping times have changed dramatically enough to turn error into success.

Climatic details present the same problem for growers, their geological cycle of a far longer time frame than the farmer's. If a grower tries to nurture a plant typically thought of as barely hardy in his zone and succeeds because of favorable weather, he might "bet the farm" on that species, then "lose the farm" when the climate goes back to a normal phase or swings to the other cusp on its Bell Curve distribution. History abounds with tales of dry farmers reaching virgin ground in an unfamiliar area, finding extraordinary yields when rains come at the right time, then failing miserably when the desert reclaims its due.

The Zen farmer, like the scientist, makes surmisals from his experience but understands their tentative nature—when *this* was done in *these* conditions *that* happened. With repeated experiments, scientists verify or disprove their hypotheses, but the farmer lacks the time to do so, not to mention finds replicability nigh impossible: two climatic years are rarely the same, likewise multiple market situations, and never do two places ever compare exactly. Whatever learning comes is always tentative.

Bateson went so far as to use man's common learning process as proof refuting Lamarckian evolution, which as a competing theory to Darwinism suggested that lessons gained by the parent passed through genes to the offspring. If Lamarckism were true, he wrote, evolution would always reach a dead end, the worlds of each generation cutting off more and more possibilities until there were none. For species to change the young must take chances and make mistakes, embrace their ignorance of the unlikely, a bad outcome usually imminent for the individual but, in the trusty form of *allos*, useful for the species as a whole. Mutations, almost all of them evolutionary cul-de-sacs, perform a similar function, nature's shotgun approach of diversity making it possible for outliers to be the survivors in unusual times and places.

Almost tit-for-tat, the old dismiss the brazen wisdom of the young just as the youthful discard the polished sagacity of the aged, though for a different reason. Having seen enough harebrained schemes, "new and improved" products that weren't, and technological saviors that complicated, rather than simplified, their world, they're quick to shut down attention when a world-shattering idea excites the young. It's the statistically correct (but illogical) thing to do.

Both groups, the young and the old, make premature decisions, a swift and necessary survival tactic in the wild (and even in "tamed" civilization) but one lacking *allos,* that touch of otherness (in this case, self-doubt) that situates an object properly among others. This partly derives from problems inherent to observation, problems troubling even physicists, who find themselves unable to measure a particle's position and motion simultaneously. Life is in flux, always moving, and while we operate with discovered knowledge the world moves on, changing the facts. We know where we are and where other things are going, or we know where other things are and where we are going, but we generally can't perceive all those motions and positions at once.

The elderly recognize *allos* but, running out of time, are quick to dismiss its contents, while the young, fascinated by difference, overly attend to it. What begins as a natural and evolutionary useful inclination, usurping the old guard and adopting new methods, creeps into the youthful worldview and attaches to all information and institutions. Mention "disruption" and you get the attention of the current generation, just as earlier catchwords captured prior eras' notice, because the mind gravitates to the unusual and anomalous, difference instantly grabbing our attention and yanking us around like a rancher pulling a mean bull's nose ring.

Stories and myths spring not from normalcy but from situations that break the common flow of life—*allos*. News organizations always sell more papers when reporting the sensational, the Internet, due to its quickness, exacerbates that tendency with its omnipresent clickbait and search for scandal. And at the farm? Instagram and the Facebook group, where we find our tribe, is filled not just with trolls but with those too much like us, often starry eyed and ill informed, spreading premature conjecture and magic potions we too easily accept, suggesting hacks for every task we clamor to use, describing enticing ways to get around the usual manner of doing things, offering remarkable gadgets to change and improve, all as alluring to the farmer as a shiny object is to a pack rat.

So the no-till farmer and the no-self acolyte, meeting at the end of the no-row, ultimately face the choice: return to the world in an impure fashion or disappear; embrace *allos* or seek to break it, evade it. From a sufficiently distant viewpoint, of course, *allos* decides for them as the only way that life can continue.

———

Kant considered time and space the only *a priori* concepts in consciousness, coming to us as innate knowledge, a framework preceding experience. All else is learned. Any gardener, any farmer, but especially the flower grower nurturing upwards of a hundred different species, must get a grip on time and space and situate himself amidst them to succeed, and all else follows from there. He must know the seasonal parameters and spatial needs of every cultivar. Timing especially proves crucial for many tasks: irrigating, harvesting, deadheading, pruning, planting, and working the ground. Too late to irrigate, he cripples the plants; too early, he weaken and drown them. Too eager to rotovate, he turns the wet earth into clods that only winters of freeze and thaw can disassemble; too late and the clay soil, already hardened and dry, refuses to yield. Leave deadheading to the last minute and, weed or flower, their spent blossoms go to seed, wasting his effort and creating extra work next year. Harvest some species too soon and they wilt, others too late and they brown. Plant before the ground warms and seedlings languish, plant when no chance of frost exists and they wither in the sun and wind. Knowing, then recognizing, and most importantly, acting when the proper moment appears makes the difference between success and failure. There is always a time window, an area in which the farmer must situate himself and his wards.

Physical spacing, too, looms important, the grower needing to know how much room each plant requires, how tall it grows, where the most advantageous place—in regards to soil make-up and shade/sun requirements—to position it is. He creates aisles suitable for transport and fitting his equipment's size. He arranges market routes to keep mileage low and for efficient distribution, places his outbuildings and coolers in convenient proximities, fixes his irrigation system areas for maximum efficiency and easiest operation. He loads the cooler and the truck in relation to pertinent variables, making sure to utilize space without wasting it. In the greenhouse, that most valuable—because most costly—space, he chooses quick growing plants and spaces them tightly, maybe leaving little room for even the slimmest workers, valuing profit over slight discomfort.

Zen involves such adjustments, as an attitude it helps situate the individual amidst a world in motion. It's not a super power, one—*voila!*—giving instant knowledge of the proper amount and type of action required in a given moment. Instead, it entails both learning and unlearning on a continual basis. You needn't *be* Zen to know your context, to know yourself, that's how you *become* Zen, and you do so through feedback, by poking the bear and feeling the bear poke you back: test, result, repeat. Simple enough, if you get through the initial response and the bear doesn't eat you. Thankfully, feedback tends not to be that drastic, leading more often to embarrassment than mauling.

Horst Mittelstaedt typologized learning methods into *feedback*, which he compared with shooting a rifle, and *calibration*, experienced when using a shotgun. You shoot a rifle high, adjust the sights, shoot low, adjust again, the third shot hitting the target—much like Goldilocks' method of finding the right porridge. The flower farmer uses the rifle method when he plants too early, plants too late, then plants in the most appropriate window of time. A shotgun and a moving target, however, allow no time for such simple adjustments. Requiring a great deal of practice, shotguns necessitate a larger set of feedback events to learn how to use them accurately.

A farmer's irrigation protocol closely follows the shotgun approach, requiring constant adjustment as weather changes, as species change, as plants grow bigger, as they prepare to bloom or go dormant. Even after years of irrigation experience, he might get caught in a mistake. The farmer learns through feedback and calibration all the time—no matter how correct his perceptions and actions are at one moment they might not fit a second one. As new information comes in, he adjusts his sights. As emergencies or contingencies arise, he recalibrates. His context determines which tools he needs, what he needs to do and how to do it.

These essential components of learning run counter to the impatient student's expectation of an *AHA!* moment to propel him from not-knowing to knowing as if he were an electron jumping from one orbit to another, with no effort from him save a passive acceptance of a benevolent teacher's offerings. Present throughout history, this tendency gets reinforced by the instantaneous technology now at hand. Finding an answer once entailed searching through encyclopedias, periodicals, textbooks, visiting with experts, apprenticing with masters, but all those journeys—a source of collateral learning acquired by osmosis along the way—have been outsourced to a click of the mouse.

Watch a YouTube video, listen to a podcast, and get the impression you know something. Google your question, forget the answer—no matter, you can always Google it again. A disconnect exists between the world and Internet user: the electronic tools give a sensation of experience but provide only copies of it. The richness of actual doing, the assimilation of understanding into one's own mind, gets lost. No matter how many podcasts one listens to, if the information isn't incorporated into actions and doesn't become permanent knowledge it equates to a storage unit possession—you have it, but it's not a part of your life.

Learning occurs at the meta-level, too, of course, but mathematical and conceptual mistakes differ from their shooting counterparts just as knowing differs from doing. You can know the physics of bicycle riding, know how to construct a bicycle, know how you're supposed to ride a bicycle, but until you ride a bicycle you've not learned to do so. The actual rider one-ups the "knower" who, despite his broader understanding of bicycle riding, doesn't know at all. Likewise, the farmer with the hoe in his hand probably has more practical knowledge than his earbud-wielding counterpart, whose theoretical knowledge, while possibly helpful, gets in the way of the physical world's feedback/calibration process.

Engineers and designers stand long accursed by commercial farmers using their products. Those off the farm have "their heads in the clouds" and consequently miss out on important details of actual use. The expression "those who can, do, those who can't, teach" reveals the same prejudice, a populist resentment against the white-collar or meta-level worker. Zen, funny enough, sits in a similar position in that it proclaims the supremacy of doing, but it lacks the anger and quick disparagement toward the knowing class—such action resides in that Serenity Prayer area of wasted effort, better instead to pay attention to one's own actions: doing.

Most farmers, while able to fashion rudimentary implements in the spur of the moment—when weekend breakdowns occur, for instance—can't engineer a tractor, mine the elements necessary to build one, forge the materials to create it, design the electronics needed to run it, despite their sense of superiority as users. Complex designing almost necessitates a mind removed from the physical world—there's just too much to think about when straddling the concrete and abstract, two separate sets of grid cells. Only a few extraordinary people operate equally well at the physical and mental levels, are able to tie flies and do calculus and bounce back and forth between the tasks. Mostly, the old stereotypes of the bookish physicist and the backwoods Mr. Fixit hold true, arising as they do from the needs of the specific arenas where they are situated.

The founding structures of time and space sink into the brain's equivalent of a storage unit, become *hintergedanken* (the thoughts in the back of your mind). A farmer might equate that place to the lower layers of a soil profile which he never pays attention to, the founding level underlying his topsoil of sand or clay or (lucky him!) loess. He might think of it as deeper yet if he read his well driller's log, past the layers of basalt, of cinder, of shale, past the even deeper water beyond which the drill bit need go no further. Space and time may strike him as interesting but immediately unimportant, though he may deem the learning and faux-learning attached to them of utter urgency.

The meta-world of ideas, words, thoughts, and emotions coats and occludes its underlying essence of time and space, is itself enveloped again and again by additional layers of self reference and meta-references. Before language, primary experience remained exposed and apparent to all, but words, even though only slightly more tangible than thought, brought internal understandings to voice. Mankind's attention quickly drifted from the actual to the referential. The same process culminates now in virtual, screen-centered reality. That version of reality may settle, too, into *hintergedanken*, replaced by the next layer of technology, a thing-about-a-thing-about-a-thing-about-a-thing, thickly encasing the meta-actual as well as the actual.

Economists often emphasize ours is a service economy, downplaying the founding sectors of mining, farming, and forestry, ignoring the obvious consideration of how short a lifespan an economy fully based on recreating, on transport, on exchanging poems, art and song might be without food, shelter, and heat. "The dumb economist" joins the "dumb farmer", joins the rest of us bound in ignorance by our refusal to note the importance of underlying features of reality.

Take the shop teacher, a couple fingers lost when he let his understanding become buried *hintergedanken* even as his expertise expanded. Look to those living off the grid, their definition of "off" as "separated from" and therefore askew, since they likely use the grid's roads, services and products, possibly sell their own products to customers on the grid—"off", then, meaning "from", in the sense of a parasite's action toward its host. The off-gridder has forgotten the fundamentals of his existence, the indisputable fact that he did not and could not build his phone, his pickup truck, or the networks necessary for them to operate.

The small farmer, wish as he might to just attend to his farm in a Zenlike manner, sowing and irrigating and harvesting, witnessing growth and decay and the movement of natural elements, must move into the meta-world of product presentation, of client relations, of business protocols and financial transactions, and in doing so lose the simplified existence he cherishes. He may be fitted for moving between such levels of being and seamlessly exchange his Zen farmer hat for his Zen salesman hat for his Zen accountant hat, but more likely he feels a chatter in his gears as he shifts from one way of action to the next.

Likely he feels hypocritical, unable to be a grower attached to his product and then a salesman when presenting his efforts to a client. The arrangements he made with nature don't really apply to the objects in the meta-worlds that surround it, those objects' rhythms and spacing faster and tighter, more erratic. Plants, soil and weather he understands, social and financial interactions perhaps not so much. Adept at one level, less so or not at all at another, he might be like the monk sent from the monastery to an overseas conference, enlightened in his natural habitat but panicky in the sudden onslaught of crowds in an airport—the monk turned around and returned to his monastery, chastened by his failure and knowing he wasn't Zen at all.

A small trailer sits behind the farm shop. Small enough to tow with a pickup but parked on blocks, its hitch exposed, outside walls dented, inside paint peeling, kitchen grimy with decades of grease, bathroom fixtures rust-colored, carpets burred and exposing underlying structure where worn, it serves as a summer work camp used by three Mexican laborers who come each spring to work. It goes empty after they leave in late October, the potato crop harvested, home beckoning, Idaho cold pushing the unprepared workers south like it does the geese and other migrating birds. One fall Margarito asks to stay to seek winter work, hoping to someday become a citizen. The trailer, walls filled with only an inch of insulation, isn't constructed for below zero weather but the farmer, grateful for Margarito's loyalty and eager to see him succeed, agrees.

As the winter deepens, other area laborers with similar dreams and equally poor success persuade Margarito to let them stay with him (without the farmer's knowledge), until nine reside in the thirty by eight foot trailer. The propane bill runs astronomically high, demanding scrutiny; the farmer discovers glass broken from a back window by those living closest to the heat vent, while those in the front, furthest from the heater, keep turning up the thermostat. Two parts of the same system working against each other, unable to reach equilibrium. Just like the dissonant human mind.

Consider the farm as a system, like Margarito's trailer, its co-owning couple (co-conspirators?) the mind that operates its parts. Bateson proposed we should think of mind as not a thing in our head but as a system, using the example of a woodsman chopping a tree down with an ax—woodsman-ax-tree exemplifies Bateson's notion of mind, as does a blind man with a cane on a sidewalk, a backhoe operator opening a bottle of beer with his shovel from a distance. Add to his examples a flower farmer with his scissors or loppers cutting his harvest—farmer-scissors-plant a unified mind. On a farm, those running it, the employees and tools of the farm, and the land and its physical components comprise a similar but larger system or mind, and if those in charge have conflicting aims, the rest of that mind will struggle.

Stilling the mind often stands primary as a Zen attribute or goal, long hours of sitting meditation a common laic impression of its character, but movement states its case, too, in the Zen no-mind. Living systems move, simple as that, their parts balanced or in full equilibrium only when they die. The mind, when oscillating like Margarito's trailer, tends toward discomfort, but even when still, in the Zen sense, experiences movement. Sociology's Symbolic Interactionists speak of that movement when they theorize that the self alternates between two parts, the acting, subjective "I" and the fixed, objective "me". The "me" is my self-impression composed not just of actual past but my unreliable appraisals, is a pendulum-swinging activity that Sartre described with a roughly corresponding set of different terms, the active and conscious *for-itself* and the static *in-itself.* The Buddhists, too, address the ineffable motion inherent in consciousness with the term *vijnana,* sometimes translated as "river of selves", that same fluid, downstream motion Heraclitus captured in his phrase "you can't step into the same river twice." No instant, no self, no river or place stays the same, all agree. And Whitehead, trying to identify that movement, coined the "occasion" as the smallest bit of subjective experience, each occasion dissipating as it becomes incorporated into the next instant—that movement loosely equating to the river of selves, though expressed in typically Western non-fluid, "billiard ball" fashion, sliced into parts akin to Ikea furniture components. The way things move and change—and don't—has yet to fully reveal itself to man but it doesn't keep him from trying to conceptualize it.

But neither the pendulum swing of the Interactionists and Sartre nor the recursive occasion, nor a constantly flowing *vijnana* require or embody the oscillation inherent to the system exemplified by Margarito's trailer, where the either/or of the pendulum gives way to the movement of a choice-less system working against itself. If the aim of philosophy, religion and psychology could be summed up in a single notion, it is that they seek to divert man from that system-roiling sensation to a calmer way of being.

As a system, a farm can operate like a healthy, independent self—the "I" and the "me" alternating, always creating new occasions, much like the way we walk with one foot planted and one foot moving forward—or it can operate instead like the trailer, when partners operating it undermine one another with directly conflicting intentions. If those aims become conscious, reach the stage of verbal battle, a normal if unpleasant state of affairs may result, but when unacknowledged those aims create an out-of-control system that vacillates crazily between incompatible states, a condition Bateson would call *schismogenetic*—directed toward collapse or a violent end. From ordering seeds to irrigating plants to working the soil to processing flowers to making sales, if one part of the farm-brain does one thing and the other part commits to its opposite, the likelihood of generating a system-ending schism increases. The controlling parts, subject to entropy, can take no more.

Many a farm spouse complains about being unable to get away from the acreage, of being married to the land and work. If the old saw about a "farm owning the farmer" describes the agricultural relationship then the growers may be drowning in that bond. The solution that most overtaxed spouses imagine uses distance to physically perform what the Serenity Prayer intends to do with the mind, provide space and a clear boundary between one level of existence and other. In itself, however, any method fails if the user refuses to use it properly—the tool is only one part of the Batesonian mind.

Judaism introduced the day of rest in part to alleviate the farmer's stress from constant toil. It provided a Sabbath of distance from work under threat of God's vengeance. The industrial age refined that split between work and play so thoroughly that a majority of the modern world still compartmentalizes the two—for decades a typical employee could switch off work on Friday at five PM, switch on vacation time until 8 AM Monday morning, and though work patterns now encompass a much broader schedule variation, the on/off treatment persists through historical acculturation and habit. The emphasis on *allos* that rest provides occasionally reaches such intensity that workers gladly return to the job for relief from having too much weekend fun. A change is as good as a rest, the cliché goes, and is never so true as when work becomes a vacation from the vacation.

The farmer's activities, bound to nature, don't lend themselves to the sort of short-term forgetfulness that allows compartmentalization—go ahead and take a vacation day but the weeds will not; the crops keep using water; a day of harvest gets lost, a portion ruined by over-ripening. The cattle rancher and the shepherd might slip away from the herd or flock, their animals able to find their own water and food, but plants prove to be a bit passive-aggressive, even suicidal, insisting you do their bidding and provide the sustenance they need. Any labor avoided in a taken respite just accumulates in the work bank, a reservoir of tasks infinitely patient for the farmer's return. It draws interest, in fact, since nature tends to grow and minor tasks expand into huge ones if not undertaken at the proper time. A sense of franticness, like that of a *boid* losing its position in the flock, may arise from being behind or outside the flow of nature, so "time away" entails catching up.

The impulse to leave an emotionally compressing situation, while a correct intuition aimed toward health, works for nomads who stay at a place until it is too befouled, then pack up and leave it behind. It works, too, for an addict or alcoholic—a primary tenet in AA literature advises the drinker to change his playmates and his playground, thus he's not tempted to imbibe when he encounters details of his past life. But for a farmer that intends to keep, rather than abandon, his business, leaving for vacation is the equivalent of a non-viable diet's cheat day, and moving off the farm is a substantial cheat distance giving him one more thing to juggle, another world to negotiate—a place of opposition, really, setting up for battle.

You can worry just as much about the farm from a distance as when you reside on it, you're just limited in your ability to remedy problems. Space away from the farm is just a variation of time away, a geographical rather than temporal solution with similar results. It only works if undertaken logically rather than from a magical viewpoint—if the farmer's methods and the farm's demands don't change, neither will the problem.

Perhaps, on your way to the airport, you suddenly can't remember if you turned off the toaster. You can't go back without missing your flight, you have no one to call to check and see, and the worry just keeps eating at you until enough time passes that the worst thing that could happen (the house burning down), if it was going to happen, has already happened. Such "toaster moments" occur regularly to the (perhaps overly) diligent, can be rectified on the farm—if you live there—by giving in to *hintergedanken*, getting out of bed and checking to see if you turned the pump off, if you closed the greenhouse doors, if you left the cooler open, if you sent the email or text. Away from the farm, free of its constant proximity, you lose the ability to fix such problems.

A Buddhist parable, while not aimed at toaster moments, nonetheless illustrates how they infiltrate the mind: two monks encounter a distressed young woman at a river, and though monks are barred from interaction with females one of them consents to carrying her across the water. Some minutes later, the other monk, taken aback by the act, asks how he could commit such a transgression. "I let the girl off back at the riverbank," he calmly replies. "But you are still carrying her." If you're a monk that can let go of his toaster moments, moving away from the farm might prove to be somewhat of a solution—but if you are such a monk, why would you need to leave?

Geographical solutions tend to be imaginary ones. Most anyone experiences that youthful inclination to "get out of this Podunk town" whether the town is a desert trailer cluster or a metropolis. Sometimes a change of scenery indeed changes a life, but more frequently an individual's nature, a set of unique features on a wobbling object with an undefined trajectory, just finds an environment corresponding to the one it left, one having a similar set of features that happens to make a snug, comfortable fit. That unconscious "fit" (dare we say *in situ?*) between objects, the counterpart of the mis-fitting allergen and host, gets shadowed by a conscious urge toward familiarity, and between the two, someone who leaves ends up right where he began—like a portion of a massive flock of ducks rising from the feeding grounds, but only briefly, before dropping down again not far from the spot they left.

A spouse in couples' therapy might refer to the partner as "emotionally distant", indicating how we perceive emotions to be placed much like physical objects, and some research indicates that we do in fact situate them with their own system of border, grid, and place cells. On a farm run by couples, each partner typically has a private, independent orbit of physical action, an area of the business he or she attends to, but also has a mental and emotional orbit tied to the partner's. Plenty of arrangements between the two lie in the realm of possibility—they can be two comets passing by on a regular, predictable trajectory, one partner can be a central sunlike figure and the other an orbiting planet, there can be combinations of cyclicality based on elliptical or perfectly circular trails, and more erratic relationships, too. Bateson typologized relationship possibilities as symmetrical or complementary, participants in the former exhibiting like behaviors (both might be tidy, for instance) and in the latter operating along opposite actions (one a spender, one frugal). Since relationships constantly change, schismogenetic outcomes always loom, with symmetrical relations escalating (ala an arms race) and complementary ones (sadomasochism, for example) likewise gaining intensity until collapse inevitably occurs. Pessimistic as such an appraisal seems, most relationships operate on multiple layers that defuse the schismogenetic tensions, with the submissive butler or office secretary often in control of scheduling and other tasks, giving them dominance in one arena that diffuses the too-great energy inherent in an escalatory relationship.

Every farm relationship differs, but all bear the possibility of tension, of a workplace with the emotional equivalent of a chattering washboard country road. Some understanding of the farm structure needs to be explicit, borders need to be drawn—but not too many lest clutter ensues and even more levels of discord arise.

———

The Zen sage rests when he is tired, eats when he is hungry. Similarly, the Zen farmer plants, irrigates, maintains his field, and harvests at appropriate times. This entails understanding plant requirements, how they are positioned in space and time, understanding the climate and soil, understanding himself and where he is positioned, too. He doesn't try to fool nature as if it was an enemy, he isn't the clever adversary, he just streamlines his tasks rather than trying to evade them via trickery, technology, or mental gymnastics. If someone doesn't like the tasks farming entails, why would he farm?

But routes do exist, often in multiple numbers and some far more circuitous than others, between the first recognition of a task and its completion, and it takes insight to quickly see the best or quickest way to do something. Some say necessity is the mother of invention and leads to this insight, but others give laziness that status. Both factions might be right, but the pathways inspired by need differ from those spawned by indolence. Having a problem that needs a solution yields one sort of thing; creating a problem when one doesn't exist and then finding a solution to it yields something else entirely. The desperate and the needy lack feasible solutions, they fumble about in a darkened abyss so grasp for immediate and simple answers to their dilemmas; the lazy have solutions, on the other hand, just find them distasteful, and thief-like they seek to bypass normal routes.

Maybe mankind always possessed the mental trigger that seeks to solve problems—his ancestor, *homo habilis* (handy man), used tools over two million years ago. But fascination with that trigger must be a recent development. A habit developed, perhaps, starting with the successful connection of seeing a problem and making it disappear, and that feeling of success, that *voila!* moment, became a focus: I want that feeling of having solved a problem, so why wait around for problems, let's hunt for or create some!

That itch to find a way out of a place we didn't know we wanted to leave, the desire to jump the queue or reorder the normal everyday flow, the urge to insert a third object between the self and the desired, to add a step to the usual progression of action, the obsession to make something already easy yet easier—we cast together all these secondary impulses along with their primary cousin, the one born of need, into the category of inventiveness though they differ greatly.

You might attribute it all to the virtue of curiosity (which killed the cat, we must remember), but neither interest in what lies behind life's veils nor discovering what does necessarily leads to interference with nature. The Greeks, after all, had the steam engine's design but chose not to implement it; South Americans didn't utilize wheels as Europeans did though they had toys that sported them; and anyone who exercises self-restraint understands that having power needn't entail using it.

Power always played a part in human interaction, but recently its vector—selfishness—has skulked into virtue status, thanks in great part to Adam Smith's capitalistic "invisible hand" that suggests self-interest, in the big picture, to be a force for societal good, opening the floodgates of egoism by erasing its negative stigma.

Inventiveness, as curiosity, might be a natural expression of humanness but inventiveness to gain power, to elevate the self to the center of reality from its status as a subset moving through a larger universe is a cultural artifact removed from the Zen ideal. That ideal includes both the cultivation of curiosity and the joy of discovery. Liken activity beyond those two things to the hunter who bags the rare animal to show family and friends. Taking the unique rather than sparing it, he wants not to share his wonder but enhance his self-worth. Such a hunter—and any farmer like him—positions himself amidst a host of social objects and fellow beings in a hierarchical arrangement based on scarcity, one he is poised atop. His universe is a lifeboat on which each individual struggles to get his share.

Oftentimes, inventor-farmers consider themselves outside the norm. Sometimes they feel ostracized or shunned, other times they feel like pioneers forging their own path, and at yet other times experience a confusing oscillation of both—ala the hot/cold warfare in Margarito's trailer. They may see themselves as aberrant saviors possessing cleverness, highly honed perceptions, and the ability to see what others don't. Even the most mundane task, then, becomes the hero's journey, and they take the fodder of possibility, churn it through their remarkable but unremarked-upon skills and abilities to create unneeded solutions for nonexistent problems. Often autodidacts, untethered to the "flock" or structures of academia or even a commonsensical canon, they are sometimes exceptionally bright in some areas and extraordinary lacking in others. Cockeyed? Hare-brained? Or prodigy?

There are farmers who tie their hands to current and past practices, those who lean on the past but keep their attention to possibility, and there are those looking for a way or tool to circumvent what is and what was, eager for the future and considering themselves trendsetters, ready to adapt. As outliers, they sometimes introduce new technology and ideas that become part of the farming canon, but as outliers they primarily serve the cultural equivalent of genetic mutations, their discoveries unusual, sometimes redundant, only occasionally useful.

So what constitutes the "good" tool and the "bad"? Wendell Berry's description of proper technology in his essay "Why I am not Going to Buy a Computer", listed his requirements (which seem more Amish than Zen): a tool should be cheaper and smaller than the one it replaces, do work demonstrably better, use less energy, be reparable by an average person with common tools, be purchasable close to home—where a support system also exists, and shouldn't disrupt anything good that presently exists, like community and family. For Berry, the tool as well as the farmer needs to be situated in the world, not trying to evade it.

A tool is a way, an ambassador between two things, a vine between two trees if you're a monkey, an ingratiating remark if you're a social climber. While some claim "it's the journey and not the destination", it's easy to get lost dawdling on that journey, easy to become fascinated with technology and to mistakenly fall for its twin, magic. Rube Goldberg made a career of satirizing the tendency, designing elaborate illustrations of machines that performed simple tasks in complicated ways. The less specialized of us get similarly diverted—creating committees to study problems rather than just solving them, for instance, or making a law to balance the budget rather than just balancing it, or buying an expensive implement for a minor but annoying task. Something alluring sidetracks attention from the entirety of a situation to its *allos,* that last little blemish of imperfection that with just a little tweaking, one thinks, will disappear. Artists call this habit "getting tight", overworking a piece by attending so much to detail that they ruin it. Farmers, too, can obsess about getting it just right when they try to figure out a way to outsmart not just nature but all the thousands of others preceding them—there must be a way to get around doing X, has to be a tool that eliminates tedious Y. If they absorb too many stories highlighting anomalies—the high school dropout who became a billionaire, the inventor who transformed the system, the scientist who saw the flaw in an accepted theory— they might pattern their actions upon those anecdotes, ignoring the thousands of dropouts who ended up in dead end jobs, inventors who tinkered their life away without success, scientists who went down rabbit holes others already thoroughly investigated.

Such attention paid to anomalies flattens the Bell Curve, expands *allos* beyond its minority status, lengthens that somewhat weed-riddled row-end toward the once cleanly hoed center. Someone overly distracted by the unusual saws off Mittelstaedt's shotgun barrel, his attention losing accuracy and scattering widely without gaining power. Yes, the unlikely is possible, but it is still unlikely—the Zen farmer acts accordingly.

It might seem that, just as the wayward farmer tries to thread the needle with clever techniques, elaborate systems, and magical tools (and even magic itself), the Zen farmer attempts to achieve an equivalent sort of elusive perfection—just a different needle, just a different thread. And, if the Zen farmer, like his cohort, perceives Zen's Middle Path, a halfway point between self-indulgence and self-mortification, as a solution, as a bright swelling of being that suddenly erases all life's difficulties, indeed his narrow aim mimics the impulse toward magic—not Zen at all. A Zen farmer, rather than grasping for method or talisman, situates himself inside the entirety of his environment between the things within it, and moves with them as a partner. He becomes, in a very real sense, that Batesonian mind-as-system. The hack-oriented farmer burrows instead into a single place, often randomly so, trying to evade the existential currents about him on one hand, feeding his impression of self on the other.

Chance plays a role here, and anyone acquainted with rural humor has heard a store of jokes with the theme of farmer as gambler. The gambler, like some farmers, wants to hit it big, land in that Bell Curve's tail, the further out the better, the winnings being bigger the more unlikely the bet. Grain elevator operators relate how, when the wheat market rises, they can't coerce growers to part with their crops, while when it's on a downswing desperate farmers clamor to sell. For some farmers, no doubt, a competitive urge drives their behavior: they want to hit the top of the market, be the smartest and shrewdest grower. But, given that not even the biggest win ever sates the gambler's craving, and not even getting the best crop price ever satisfies a farmer, the process of anticipation must be the real draw.

Procrastinators try to thread the needle, that eye of the Yin and the Yang, when they wait until that last moment before the deadline to complete a task. It's a gamble without risks early on, the odds against them increasing as unlikelihood becomes impossibility. The reward of being done doesn't increase with the odds, but the adrenaline rush of beating the system heightens.

The flower farmer who tries to hit the perfect moment to plant, to deadhead, to weed, to harvest, feeds at the gambler's table, too, and suffers or prospers accordingly. Why postpone a task if doing it now presents certainty and solves the problem, other than a need to feel that adrenaline rush of being a winner, getting the correct answer, the highest price—a rush little different, perhaps, than that felt by the hacker who solves a problem he created.

A primary mistake when deciding when to start or complete a task comes not from paying too little attention but too much. Oftentimes the most focused farmer zeroes in on a particularity, and doing so loses the feedback the rest of the world offers him. Intent on harvesting every last bloom, the flower farmer ignores unharvested plants going to seed—they will become weeds next year. He neglects to see the once small weeds he left that now approach maturity—he assumed, with good intentions, he'd plow them under before they reached seed stage, but because he's threading the harvest needle he fails to do so. He waits, knowing he has plenty of time, to clean up his field in the fall. Let the perennials gain extra growth, let the annuals provide cover for birds for a while, let that cover retain extra moisture that tilling or mowing might encourage to evaporate. Focusing on the particular task, he loses sight of the larger context: if an early snowstorm falls, fall mowing becomes impossible; if the ground freezes, tilling no longer can occur; a death in the family or an illness of his own removes him from the equation; if his equipment fails, he'll have no time to fix it. The Zen farmer seizes the moment; he sees the open window and goes through it. Why wait, other than to inflate the self?

The tool is a journey, then, and any journey presents ample opportunity to deviate from the path and get lost. Though "all roads lead to Dublin" might be the practiced adage given to strayed tourists in Ireland, some roads fray and fork and run in ribbons as tangled as a discarded, knotted kite string—and some are dead ends. The Zen farmer, his attention direct, uses tools only as needed, and doesn't manufacture need where there is none. He may still wander, take a meandering path at times, but only in service of *allos* as a subset of the larger world.

Consider yourself lost on your journey if talking about how you'll do a task takes longer than doing it. Farmers with big ideas used to haunt the local grocery store and coffee shop, most of them retired, failed, or failing. They likely spent a great deal of time as a child planning games, events, small conquests with all the plans coming to naught when the dinner bell rang.

Consider yourself lost if a tool adds a step to your work. If it takes longer to do a task using it. A great rule of thumb: anytime the things-surrounding-the-thing (in this case, the-tools-surrounding-the-task) take more space, time, or resources than the thing itself, you've strayed too far—back up and start from the basic, immutable thing. When salt-of-the-earthers poke fun at academics, they inherently understand how easy it is to wander away from reality—ignoring, of course, how far and how frequently they themselves stray, though in far more unprofitable directions than education.

If a technology sends you down a cul-de-sac, consider yourself lost. When it forces you to develop a dependency upon it, take a page out of evolutionary theory to see extinction looms ahead—specialization, like that of the panda which almost exclusive eats only bamboo, generally ends badly, whereas diverse creatures like coyotes and cockroaches live on through changing times. A piece of equipment might seem to be the perfect labor-saving device, but if your whole operation depends upon its continuous well-being then a single, even small event may prove to be calamitous. A minute tweak of conditions takes many an enterprise down—you likely noticed that power outages cripple your local megastores, transactiona an eighteenth century schoolboy performed in his head unable to be completed without a computer. To rely on a single thing—a single implement, a single species, a single buyer, a single source of information, a single plant or seed source—creates an easily breakable organizational structure.

Tools, though things themselves, are in the realm of things-surrounding-the-things, residing in the same universe as talk and ideas. They're parasites, in a sense, requiring a host, not really existing without something to work on. Though we generally think of the self as an original entity, it too resides in that meta-realm, doesn't initially exist until physical events occur for it to reference, though as experience accumulates a complexly layered "thing" often evolves, having sensations about experiences, then thoughts about sensations, then thoughts about those thoughts, but all still attached like barnacles to direct experience.

That world of the self may be the favorite part of life for most of us. Drama. Rumor. Gossip. The promise. The argument. Choosing. And then there is the persona, that circus tent of the self we continually work at, propping up one pole as another falls. It's a sagging canvas, a mask that others witness. Or you can imagine it as a bag—a meta-bag, the bag stuffed with the other bags you bring home from the grocery store. Try to bring in your purchases without one, find how useful as a tool a bag with a handle is, how a simple conceptual invention changes the flow of everyday existence. A self is a bag— look at the bag-less animals, see how they can sometimes string things together but lacking a bag for the most part can't, their memories present but, without that bag-self, appearing random and unconnected, needing to be rekindled every morning and sometimes repeatedly throughout the day.

The self is a tool, a string connecting occasions, and was perhaps always part of human existence. But its use exploded after Descartes' "I think, therefore I am", expanded again when Adam Smith freed it from vicedom, and now exponentially proliferates as a force in the selfie age. Today, no moment goes by without its thing-about-the-thing, its chronicling, its wrapper, with consultants and industry cheerleaders encouraging farmers to present a public face through Facebook, Instagram, and other platforms, to package oneself as a brand. "Tell your story", they say, meaning "put yourself in a bag."

Creating an image through social networking presents the same problems for today's flower farmer as earlier, computer-less processes did for all humans through the centuries: the split between essence, what you feel yourself to be, and appearance, the mask you wear and the face you show, results in either a Janus-like, two-fold existence you somehow become comfortable with or a dissonant sense of fraudulence that disturbs you. The Zen farmer ignores the split, pays no mind.

While, due to the nature of human perception, there is no escape from, on the one hand, *being* and on the other *being seen*, you can control only your own, not others', actions and perceptions. Manipulating a public presence easily spirals into obsession with packaging and an increasingly loose grasp on one's "true" self. Any action, self-appraised beforehand in order to judge how others might view it, turns inauthentic—you become the puppeteer behind the scenes manipulating your puppet (your "brand"). You're letting a pre-conceived notion, your public image, fix your behavior, and you're treating yourself as an object to be sold. The self, useful as a tool at times, when overly attended to sends you down a path away from your goal. Better to be a cat without a bag than a human carrying too many.

One's story, then, ideally needs to be neither bigger nor smaller than what it refers to and should match it in character, with the best narrative, of course, being no-narrative—what, besides the facts, requires telling? Let others operate as witnesses and judges. Outsource that work. Telling your story takes precious energy to inflate what happens, to create a persona, to be liked, to make a package others wish to open. It can only lead to psychological distress: if others are liking your persona, they aren't really liking you, are they? The sense of fraudulence that results can spawn a cynical outlook, a safe ironic stance that places the fraudster outside the relationship between his persona and his followers. While this may make life more interesting it makes it less Zen.

The farmer's acts, when growing, when selling, when conducting himself with others, contain his story. It isn't for him to re-tell, but for others to hear and see authentically. The good storyteller doesn't refer to his feelings as the story progresses, his feelings and character come through his inflections and gestures which act as a subtext. Such a story often lacks the hook of a savvy, polished presentation that follows a tried formula, but if you want long term customers, give them a long term story—do you want to be the pop song that everyone buys but forgets or the more complex music that took time to understand but lasted for decades? Appearance is a tool that without audience proves useless, but without essence it is a package without contents.

———

At the row's end there must be a genetic trigger that prevents perfection, that stops completion, that says "wait a minute, shouldn't we leave just a little doubt, a little possibility, a seed of sorts for alternative paths?" Mercy, you might call it, a last second reprieve at the end of the row for unwanted species, those orphans called weeds. Maybe it's akin to a car's "California stop", a slowing roll, a slight braking, but never a full rest at the stop sign, instead just a knowing nod of semi-respect. Or, is it a character flaw that needs to be beaten out: slothfulness, a sloppy work ethic, sheer boredom, or resentment and a consequent rebellion toward the boss, be it the paymaster or life itself? In any case, there it is, a drift from order into chaos.

Zen artists embrace that chaos, that imperfection, by intentionally leaving a slight crack in their pottery or a barely askew brush stroke in a painting. Tibetan Buddhists echo that homage to nature's transitoriness in their sand mandalas, painstaking artworks composed of colored sand that when finished are immediately dismantled. If dandelions, salsify, and milkweed fruited simultaneously, floral designers could make a similar bow to impermanence, could carefully arrange the airy seed heads and then let them explode when struck by breath or breeze.

In lieu of that appropriate honoring act, the designer employs a different tactic to evade the boredom of sameness and perfection. She plays with the symmetry of an arrangement, works the wiggle room that *allos* allows before something interesting becomes something strange or ugly. Rather than using "the roundy moundy" style of a formalist, the Zen designer normalizes a loose look by using an odd texture given by a seedhead, by inserting a spiked flower with a curved stem, by attaching a hanging or trailing vine, by pulling the petals from a flower and just using the central disc, by cutting a pod in half to expose its intricate center, or by giving a highly contrasting (but not clashing) display of colors—anything "different" that might fascinate the viewer.

Any designer situates herself in a historical process of changing trends, and if informality currently prevails she prospers, while when formalism has favor she becomes *allos*. A tipping point occurs at some point, perhaps when the population of formalists shrinks to five percent of the whole and thus makes the informalist common, transforming symmetry into *allos*, the unusual, the desired, and order triumphs over chaos for its turn in the limelight.

Since flower farmers need to be aware of designer trends, they too must situate themselves in historical and social developments. But saddled with temporal and spatial requirements of the physical world, their nimbleness suffers. A designer can shift styles, if not reputation, in a moment while a farmer's shrub planting takes three years to discover if he can grow it, five to get a feel for its popularity. Perennials in favor for years may go out of style—plow them under and plant a new set of species that won't flower for at least two years, long enough for them to lose popularity, too. Even annual crops lag a year behind, while trends can pivot as quickly as a viral video.

So the "color of the year"—a top down, hierarchical proclamation issued pre-season without consumer input—means little to the flower farmer, perhaps resulting in a slight tweak of plans, a minor shift of cultivar choices. And the latest bridal bouquet on the cover of a trendy magazine doesn't change what he plants this year—after all, he can't provide the spring flowers shown on the August issue of a magazine. His actual customers, not that nebulous virtual area of chat, rumor, information and misinformation (the meta) that swarms like columns of predatory mosquitoes, dictate his planting array. His awareness fixes accordingly.

The Serenity Prayer guides a grower. If his customers extend nationwide, national trends are his field of action, but he pays more attention to orders trickling in than to Internet and print buzz. If his clientele base reaches only a region, he may glance at larger trends, but looks to local nuance—a large Asian population might indicate a need for traditional marigolds, a crop elsewhere lacking market value. The Prayer, if followed, grants the grower the wisdom to ignore larger trends and pay attention instead to those closer to him.

Growers who play into information distributed too widely, or even those listening too intently to those they admire, may get inaccurate representations of what's going on—the *boids* in their vicinity may be closer or more distant than they think, may be moving in a different direction and at a different speed than told, and hence the grower might, without even knowing it, be lost.

———

That five-percent of the Yin-Yang *allos* shows up in many farmers in the eye-crossing "hack". The hack is one version of a tradition extending so far back in history that it seems DNA inspired: the urge to "get one over" on a competitor, be it a species, nature in general, society or a fellow human. As a way to beat the system, to cut corners, to bypass regular routes and methods, it seems more prevalent than ever before. All farmers, new ones especially, perhaps appraising themselves as inherently smarter than those who came before them, seem to aim for the crack in reality that makes a task easier, one that magically transforms displeasing work into an elegant experience of art.

If you tease this tendency apart you find man's historically sprawling fascination with technique, attaching first to magic and later to machines and technology. Shamans, alchemists, astrologers—take a look at their claims, prophecies and promises, substitute their potions and talismans with apps and gadgets, and you get the identical but modern obsession with the hack. Often the hack turns a simple procedure into a Rube Goldberg production, adding a step or an instrument to a process in an attempt to bypass the normal routine. A believer in love with his discovery, of course, won't see he's created confusion and complexity, just as his skeptical Luddite cousin, a technology doubter, refuses to see when a hack truly benefits the innovator.

A Zen farmer falls somewhere between technological love and hate. He never forms a sycophantic love for a tool, but appreciates what it can do in the proper hands at the appropriate moment. You might say just as a farmer has his individualized *dharma*, something akin to a calling or purpose in life, a tool has its, as well, and the principles of right action, right living, right duty, and right direction, applies to the tool as it does to the farmer. Scale enters his judgment immediately, giving him a quick assessment that eliminates tools that don't fit a context. A bed-shaper would be nice to have—but he lives in a dry climate where the soil rarely suffers poor drainage. A mechanical transplanter would alleviate those backaches when setting in spring seedlings—but it only takes a few hours each year to do the task by hand. An accurate seeder, though expensive, would eliminate waste and plant more evenly—but seeds cost little and his applicator price is a fraction of the fancy one. A chopstick or random weed stalk pries out plugs from their tray, so the clever device that removes the entire batch at once seems to be overkill. He removes his lust for an elegant solution, checks the impulse to perceive process as problem, those variables thus not dwarfing and contorting his judgment as they do the excited hacker's.

A Zen farmer, unhindered by a tool's narrow definition, might when necessary use a wrench as a lever or hammer, a screwdriver as a pry bar, a length of twine to substitute for a broken windshield wiper motor, or use a dime to turn a screw. Its dharma, like his, allows for flexibility. He doesn't need a probe to test soil moisture, just sticks his finger or hand into the ground to feel it—that's what his senses are for. As useful as irrigation timers may be, a clock works just as well, an inquisitive walk through the field being watered works even better. He needn't upload his business data to the Cloud using multiple apps, it's on paper that can be mislaid but never disappears into the ether. He uses a finger instead of a dibbler, a trowel when the soil's too hard to penetrate with his hands, a tiller when his acreage gets too large for a shovel, a tractor when too large for a tiller, lamenting just a smidgen, perhaps, that the society he's born to doesn't allow smaller scale activity to live within it comfortably.

The Zen farmer understands that *having* a tool is only a minor component of using it properly. Whatever magic it possesses comes only from using it as intended, its ownership not being a panacea. Take flower netting, for instance, an innovation that has rescued many a flower crop from the elements. A grid of 6" square, thin plastic "wires", if used properly it supports stems so that wind, rain, or sheer foliage volume doesn't topple a crop. But many a new farmer, in love with the hack, buy and use it without understanding the principles behind its success. They bought it. They have it. They put it up. Why doesn't it work?

Every object has a field of connections surrounding it: material thresholds, ranges of use, etc. Tools often don't come with an owner's manual, they assume your understanding of their use, and so it's your job to discern their characteristics. Tools like the crescent wrench ("adjustable" wrench in most countries), though no doubt mysterious to the toddler who has yet to see it in action, has such a long history and operates with such ease that manufacturers forego explanation. More specialized tools, like netting, likewise assume a purchaser skill level, and often are so versatile that a manual could not cover its possible uses. Such tools don't just automatically "fit" a specific user's understanding, but an overly confident purchaser, buoyed by a history of successful tool use, often assumes he instantly knows. Wrong.

Just as two by fours in a house frame require nails and proper fastening, must be put together in a fashion conforming to the laws of physics in order to function, netting supports only if it, in turn, is supported. Were its grids metal instead of flexible plastic, it would constrain stem movement with less support (some flower growers consequently use rolls of wire fencing for longterm crops for this reason, and others bend 8' construction panels into an upside-down "U" shape—giving them "legs" and a "table"—as a more mobile alternative), but pliable netting stretches side-to-side and back-and-forth. Even with posts interspersed every four feet down each side to support it, weather and plant mass works at its weakness. Less staking than that increases its susceptibility to movement, more staking (if properly done—it can't just be there, it has to be sturdy) lessens it. Stapling the netting to a board at the row's end, then nailing the board to well-set posts, limits lengthwise stretching. Yet more caveats: net placed too high allows stems to buckle beneath it, placed too low and stems topple above it; extra tall or heavily foliaged species often require a second layer of netting placed a foot or more above the lower one; and, the netting should be eyed regularly just to check the quality of the construction crew's work.

So much to know about a simple technology, so much more than merely buying and having it. And the lesson holds for every piece of equipment. How about the scuffle hoe, a fine invention abiding by the low-impact rule of farming? The flat style hoe most gardeners use churns up soil as it cuts at weeds, bringing up a new set of seeds lurking below, while the scuffle hoe, hoop-shaped with an empty center (somewhat like a cheese slicer), slides beneath the soil like a filet knife, cutting root systems without disturbing seeds below. But a scuffle hoe used less deftly and with excess force disrupts the soil as much as the standard instrument, rendering its primary advantage moot. The tool itself is not magic, having it in hand doesn't undo a sloppy operator's efforts. It requires understanding of its guiding principle and a submission to its limitations.

A long list of implicit, unsaid instructions attaches to even a successful hack. Owning netting doesn't make it work, your skills do. Buying an app doesn't guarantee it works for you if you fail to apply it properly. A timer starts and stops the irrigation system automatically, but it doesn't check the soil for moisture—and it doesn't monitor itself for accuracy. Any technology, by itself, is not magic, though the way you wield it sometimes approaches such— if only in an aesthetic way.

Part of the hack mentality derives from millennia of magic belief. Even prior to science and systematic logic, man made connections between cause and effect, always snagging a solution though rarely a correct one. Early man often invoked spiritual causes and attributed magical attributes to plants or talismans, omens or superstitions. Even after the Greeks developed logic (and in part, *because* of Aristotle's closed system thinking), mankind continued to start with answers, conveniently filling in the missing blanks to prop up his mental comfort, rather than observing facts and developing workable theories from them.

Magic evolved especially in the West into the love of technique, the belief that a machine, a substance or a technology would solve what society termed to be a problem. It's as if cultural attention evolved to focus on the tool segment (the ax) of the Batesonian mind of man-ax-tree, erasing and conveniently forgetting nature (the tree component). Cheap coal was the new wood that would solve energy shortage problems, cheap oil was the new coal to solve the limitations of coal, cheap nuclear was the magical answer to alleviate high costs of fossil fuel energy—rarely a day in the news goes by without a new technological advance, be it electronic, mechanical or medical, hyping itself as the solution to society's ills. How many years has nuclear fusion been touted as "just around the corner"? At least since 1965. How long have stem cells been the answer to Alzheimer's? Going on thirty years. What about the industry-transforming ceramic carburetor in Popular Mechanics in the eighties? The list is endless—take an inventory of magic solutions available now and check your findings in a year, you'll never fall for new and improved again.

Those skeptical of panaceas get labeled Luddites, curmudgeons, or worse, are simply dismissed. But the full blown Luddite and the technology or magic lover, though opposites, share one trait: they have closed systems, neither doubting themselves or their worlds the way they doubt their opposites, and neither absorbing feedback that might prove them wrong. Where does that leave us, how do we solve that closedness? How about opening that Taoist fish eye—leave the door ajar for the five percent possibility that you are wrong. That a new thing isn't necessarily bad, isn't necessarily world-saving, that an old way of doing business isn't necessarily worthless, just as it isn't necessarily necessary.

Chogyam Trungpa, a well known meditation master credited with bringing Tibetan Buddhism to the West, once noted how Americans were susceptible to grasping at any new religion, first adopting it wholeheartedly and then dropping it when the next one came along. He termed it "spiritual materialism", suggesting it to be a transferal of the American consumer template, buying and disposing of commodities, to religion. You might recognize the same template adopted by those quick to try diets, each new one replacing the last. Or those suffering from the latest disease or malaise trending in medical news. Or, in farming, those eager to adapt the latest technology or method, wishing to be the first with the new, shiny toy. Or species. There are plenty of ways besides accumulating money to chase prestige.

———

Oftentimes you can look to the end of the row in mid growing season to scout for the prevalence of pests. In the alter-ecology of the roadside, the canal bank, the fenceline, or neighboring pasture, insect populations brew at a different rate than on your farm. Consider the process as akin to water seeking its own level, and though you plunge your finger down in your acreage to keep pest numbers at bay, the surrounding waters eventually work into that space. If you manage your insects and neighbors don't, their problems spread to you, and if they do and you don't, the opposite occurs. The same holds true, of course, for weeds—you need no scientific instrument to assess the prevailing wind patterns, just look at your Canadian thistles growing to the lee of the neighbor's prolific patch—or, look at the neighbor's dandelions blooming downwind from you, courtesy of your negligence.

So, ease being a general method toward success throughout the natural world, aphids take the simplest path from neighboring areas, particularly those untended, after depleting resources there, and into your field, usually stopping at the nearest plants that fit their tastes. The underside of a sunflower leaf looks nice, but if you've been remiss in your weeding a sowthistle (*Sonchus oleraceus*) appears even more appetizing—almost any soft-stemmed plant does. Annual nightshade (*Solanum*) rides high on the list, as does bindweed, but other plants will do. Sometimes a group aphid flight lands at a significant point of difference, perhaps mistaking the gray leaves of a plot of Silver King (*Artemisia ludoviciana*) for something else they prefer, but once finding it distasteful they soon move elsewhere. Mmm, sedum. Honeysuckle!

A milkweed, *Asclepias perennias*, its white and pink forms both usable as cuts, draws orange oleander aphids (*Aphis nerii*) some years, a species otherwise leaving most flower species alone—though attacking wheat fields with a vengeance. With a bumper crop of lupine comes an equally sumptuous crop of wooly aphids, which ruin the blooms for market and sometimes kill a plant. Long before spring's last frost, another species of aphids attacks viburnum and dogwood buds, causing leaf distortion later in the season and ruining flowers. An unversed grower might be perplexed when either snowball or lacecap blooms emerge crispy and browned and he finds no insects—the aphids left weeks before, leaving only a farewell note, curled leaves and distorted blossoms their trail of damage.

A Zen farmer watches the end of the row, eyes the particular species, but does so with knowledge gained by botanists' tedious work and his own acquired experience. The botanists' work he knows to be more trustworthy than his, it having survived peer review and likely many decades of observation, trials and replication. His own? Well, he realizes one life, one moment, represents a very small sample, so if an outbreak of spider mites happens his first season he doesn't prematurely surmise it will every year. If his tulips avoid the botrytis called "tulip fire" (for its rapid sweep through a crop) for years, he doesn't assume that, because he lives in a dry climate, his crop will never suffer that affliction. Conditions, climatic and otherwise, constantly shift, and he moves ever vigilant between those conceptual objects, a *boid* in that particular flock.

At the field's edge, somewhat larger members of the animal kingdom slip into the farmer's mini-ecosystem— deer, elk, and moose eat their preferred species, often just a morsel here and a bud there, enough to ruin a crop, while trampling the species they don't eat but which are in the way. Beavers slip up from waterways to have a go at the poplar windbreak, develop a taste, too, for black walnuts as an appetizer. Other rodents find the pantry, enough rabbits and hares some years, voles and mice others, to test a vegan's non-violent philosophy. Squirrels move the tulip bulbs, though somehow evading poisonous daffodils. And then there are cougars and bears for those lucky enough to live in their midst, making harvesters question night-cutting when their headlamps catch a set of eyes in the dark, not that far away and staring directly at them at waist-level.

And diseases spread, knowing no border—a blight here, a fungus there, coming in from a hundred miles upwind and gaining a foothold if conditions prove prime. Or how about *Cercospora,* afflicting Bells of Ireland (*Molucella*) during humid periods, but arriving on seed and plugs from far across the country. A Zen farmer keeps an eye out for small outbreaks he might be able to circumvent, throws in the towel when he knows the problem is multi-county wide.

Seeds from the neighbors' fields creeps in to the ends of the rows, particularly small and light ones like purslane (*Portulaca oleracea*) or kochia (*Bassia scoparia*) easily carried by the wind, but also those with clever dispersion strategies, like wings or parachutes, that aid movement through the air. Or those with hooks like hounds tongue (*Cynoglossum officinale*), Velcro-inspiring cocklebur (*Xanthium strumerium*), goats-head (*Tribulus terrestris*), and hornseed that grab onto animals moving through them, then drop wherever chance takes them, *in situ* their motto. Birds, too, do their best to spread nature's wealth, their dispersal tactics more random, defecating bryony (*Bryonia alba*) and chokecherry seeds wherever they might perch without consideration for the farmer.

Not just at the ends of rows but at the row's edges, another threat from underground. The roots of some plant species are fibrous and rhizomatous, spread rapidly beyond their initial home. Other species with taproots might be said to be more *in situ*-inclined, in that transplanting increases in difficulty as plants mature, while the fibrous, rhizomatous species move easily, are comfortable everywhere, often thriving without the farmer's aid, some vigorous enough to resurrect from very small root bits, an ability making tillage counterproductive since it spreads, rather than controls, the species. Rhizome producers send roots out for great distances, their Lewis-and-Clark tendency posing problems for the farmer and testing his philosophical leanings. At some point, control looms necessary, the natural inclinations of mint, of *Physalis*, of *Lysimachia clethroides*, of yarrow bullying nearby species as efficiently as dreaded bindweed (*Convolvulus arvensis* AKA morning glory).

How to control, when to control—in what way does the Zen farmer insert, even impose, himself into nature's dance? Lacking hard and fast rules, he assesses the context and acts accordingly. How much of a problem can he live *with*, knowing the offending species lacks *withness* in the context of his enterprise. He perceives the potential difficulty long before difficult comes, but acts only when necessity arises, when without immediate action the problem reaches an insurmountable stage.

What does he do? Well, if he accepts Corinthians as a biblical guide then "all things are permissible" (though not beneficial), but Buddhists intend to do as little harm as possible. Hence, his method entails a light touch. He mulches if he has cheap, available material. If tillage works—which in the case of rhizomatous species, it doesn't—he tills or he pulls or hoes, if not he uses chemicals (which don't always work, either), and if any method requires constant attention or application he abandons the task. As one part of man-ax-tree, as one segment of man-business-nature, he tries to keep all components in balance and not give one of them supremacy over the others.

More colorful than most compost piles, the flower farmer's exposes his undersold, his overharvested and his mishandled. There's no hiding five hundred tulips flashing yellow, red and purple out behind the barn, no way to conceal a thousand bright-colored bug-riddled dahlias. A business school graduate might immediately mark the evidence in a spreadsheet column demanding action, his dogmatic mantra being: decrease waste and increase profit!

But waste is natural. The rule of *allos* holds—a loss of roughly five percent, perhaps—similar to the biblical tithe of ten percent, or the Koranic version, *zakat*, of 2.5 percent, a mark of slack, of flexibility, in the way we live and operate. If no flowers end up on the compost heap, you might consider yourself clever, having perfectly matched harvest and sales. You've threaded the needle, got your A+. But what about the sales you missed out on because you failed to have a surplus?

The business world reveres efficiency, cutting office workers who answer phones and service customers in order to maximize time usage and minimize cost—creating lines at the cash register and lengthening caller hold time, pushing the inefficiencies inherent in any exchange away from the business and onto the consumer. Brick and mortar stores, aided by computers, worship efficiency by limiting backroom inventory—excess inventory being a waste of capital—since with the click of a mouse they can have what you need on the next truck later in the week. But doing so, they again push the inefficiencies away from the business and on to the customer, who has to wait or go to an alternative outlet.

Power grids get unified, schools get consolidated, all in the name of efficiency—but the resultant structures become dependent on a single model of authority, and one mistake, instead of taking down one electrical area or one school, take down the entire grid, the entire school system. The Covid supply chain disruption displays how efficiency, while astonishing when everything works well, fails when even small perturbations in action alter the flow of goods. It's an old problem, visible in any sport: the athletic, remarkably trained team blows away their stodgier competitors, until their practiced, unearthly flow, perhaps just a bit too precious, gets even slightly disturbed—the imperfect plodders then become victors, being more flexible though less athletic and less aesthetically pleasing in their exploits.

Saving, the supposed virtuous solution to waste, sometimes comes close to clinging, an anathema to Zen. "Letting go" is a primary Zen tenet, one fitting on a "middle path" akin to the Greeks' notion of virtues. They, unlike modern day Westerners, viewed the virtues as sitting midway on a spectrum, with too much courage, for instance, becoming foolishness and too little turning to cowardice. When the virtue of frugality edges into miserliness it becomes a vice, just as tenacity turns to stubbornness and temperance transforms into excessive self-restraint. The farmer with a "bone pile", that heap of old parts behind the shop, exercises frugality if the pile's components consist of items usable in the near future, but if he holds on to them knowing they'll likely never be of use he's just being miserly. Clingy.

Present times, when many technological items become intentionally obsolete almost instantly, differ from eras when holding on to every scrap made economic sense. Then, a piece of metal, twine or wood might easily be repurposed by even a minimally talented farmer, while their equivalent today, the electronic component, eludes the abilities of all but the specially trained. In a world where products possess short lives by intent, keeping those no longer used or broken makes no sense—better to pass them on immediately to someone in the pipeline while they still have use.

Waste comes in many forms, and you can stretch the notion to include less obvious illustrations. Capitalism, it might be said, thrives on waste, in that it collapses needs and wants into a single category, with bread, clothing and housing equivalent to Happy Meal toys and glitter. More economic transactions mean greater the societal good, never mind collateral impacts like resource depletion. A strictly devout Protestant might deem any luxury a waste (so long as they were not selling that luxury), the flowers in the table vase a useless display of energy and time. A Zen adherent might dial that extreme version back a bit with a dose of *allos*, considering that a luxury, while certainly unneeded, stands as a detriment only if it compromises the system, be it the self, community or farm that utilizes it. Abundance need not be profligacy.

Unused space isn't necessarily wasted space, for instance. Consider the spaces between words, a relatively new introduction (about 1000 AD) to literacy. Before that "invention", scribes ran words together, not wanting to waste precious parchment or leather and making reading difficult by our standards. A bit of space between species or cultivars in the field allows for a distinct border that makes for easy discernment by even the untrained—the scabiosa starts here, after the space that follows the rudbeckia. But using space unwisely is a waste, though discerning so always comes in a context of set parameters—wide aisles to walk in waste space in one sense, but if created knowingly for comfort aren't a waste at all. Empty space needn't be wasted—Lao Tse noted that the empty hub completes the wheel, a cup's empty space provides its use.

Leaving a few flowers in the field seems a waste to the miserly, but gleaning them wastes time better spent harvesting a crop in plentiful bloom. Letting a client slide on a small bill might be deemed wasteful until you factor in time spent calling or invoicing and the possibility of losing favor with her. And if she goes out of business owing you a couple thousand dollars, think of it as a discount on the hundred thousand dollars she spent over the years you dealt with her, not a waste at all.

The word "waste" originates from a Latin word "*vastus*" meaning uncultivated, a root that also evolved into "vast". Waste infers uselessness, but a desert wasteland to a coyote, a sage grouse, or the hundreds of other animal species present, to a cedar, a sagebrush, a rabbit brush, or the five hundred other indigenous plant species, is not useless at all. When we speak of waste we rarely do so objectively, it being always tied to a subjective context. The compost pile, waste to the marketing farmer, won't be wasted from nature's point of view, will instead be consumed and redistributed in other forms. Just as the Serenity Prayer exemplifies different perspectives of local and within-reach as opposed to global and out of one's purview, any definition of waste depends on the witness' point of view.

———

At the end of the row you find where your irrigation water last trickles. Flood irrigators, an increasingly rare breed, display their character and abilities here. But the lay of the terrain and the nature of the soil, combined with the parameters of the stream at the row's head, limit his talents' reach. On a surface with very little slope, in possession of a slowly flowing ditch, he might dribble water equivalent to a garden hose stream that takes 24 hours to get to the row's end three hundred feet from its beginning. It might be a point of pride to irrigate so gently as to need no irrigation boots to keep one's feet dry, an equally prideful result when no ponding occurs at the row's end as it does at his neighbor's. But the consequence of his attention to his art soaks the soil at the head too thoroughly, the time roots spent steeping in water far greater than that experienced by their row's end counterparts. Those receiving first get too much water; those receiving last get too little.

Farmers sometimes say it's like "being a Catholic at the end of a Mormon ditch" to cover the misfortunes that result from being in the wrong place, in the wrong time. The group disparaged is interchangeable, of course, dependent on the speaker's allegiance. The last in line. The dirty end of the stick. Upstream, there's plenty of water, but each irrigator along the ditch takes his share, leaving the end user with whatever remains. Not always enough. The flow at his place is far less vigorous, evaporation having taken its portion, and every square foot down the ditch's length gets what it needs to soak the soil, weeds and grass of its banks. Too, the neighbors' errors collect at the last shareholder's acreage—poorly maintained banks, gopher and mouse holes draining small amounts of water, cattle hooves eroding ditch integrity, along with intentional miscalculations and sheer, if occasional, malicious theft.

Other problems accumulate, too, like weed seed that rides the water and disperses on his land, eager to germinate in coming years. Winter trash blown in the ditch from upstream neighbors floats his way—plastic bags and cardboard, insulation and light bits of construction material, candy wrappers and occasional plastic toys. Some years, when the river gets managed just so and the stars align, trash fish decide to come downstream.

Occasionally, on a Sunday when upstream churchgoers truncate their irrigation without notifying the ditchrider, an excess amount overflows the banks onto his crops. The water itself doesn't defy prediction, being subject to natural law, but the users' laws prove to be flexible and their actions difficult to forecast.

But it's water, which he'd not have without a ditch.

The "Tao" is sometimes called "the watercourse way", emphasizing life's fluid like qualities, unlike westernized descriptions of life (which, not surprisingly, arose in relatively waterless, desert conditions) focusing on life's solidity, certainty, and separateness. A farmer, bound to his livelihood by both the solidity of soil and the fluidity of water, often experiences a curious melding of two opposing philosophies—unless he's Taoist, in which case he enfolds the two as a single interwoven process.

Water and soil—a hydroponic grower likes his the equivalent of a blank slate, a filtered water free of disease and a "soil" stripped to its bare minimum, a sterile medium to support plant roots. He sends scientifically generated amounts of nutrients normally present in soil through the water to feed the roots, leaving no waste and eliminating many problems usually associated with growing. Large-scale commercial farmers wish for but don't get something similar, since native soils harbor pathogens, some indigenous but some a result of over-farming and under-rotating crops.

Idaho farmers often quote the late potato mogul J.R. Simplot, a billionaire who started his fortune by selling dehydrated product to the government for WWII troops, as saying the best crop rotation for spuds was "a thousand years of sagebrush and one of potatoes." Species often thrive most in just such shocks to the system, when they inhabit the position of *allos,* their surprise appearance sending nature's routine into momentary stasis. Bacterial, fungal, viral and insect pressures, ready for the same battles they've been engaged in for millennia, in general respond slowly to new entities, but just as a rock thrown in a pond makes a momentary crater that rapidly fills, the surrounding biome that initially fails to respond to an intrusion evolves to incorporate the new species, developing strategies and introducing pests to take advantage of the fresh resource, fight the upstart enemy.

"In situ" runs into trouble here, the potato suited to the place it was planted but certainly not native, the area's soil amenable for its growth, the climate's hot days and cool nights fitting its needs, its humidity low enough to inhibit most fungal and bacterial growth but its aridity ultimately a deal-killer—without the farmer to apply water, not many Idaho localities would be growing potatoes. In a wetter climate, like Ireland's, potatoes thrive—until they don't, the Great Famine a testament to the dangers of

not just humid climates like Ireland's, which fostered the blight that destroyed potato crops and resulted in millions starving to death and millions migrating to other countries (including the United States), but also the inherent problem of monocropping, almost all of the afflicted Irish potato crop a single cultivar that offered no resistance to the disease.

You might consider inserting water into an arid region, a fairly early experiment using nature as a palette, an equivalent to introducing a non-native species to an area. Either action affects outcomes much as changing the gears in a transmission, which alters torque and speed, or similarly shifting a cog on a grain drill, the desired spacing of the dropped seeds widening or drawing closer in accordance with the species being planted. No ecosystem conforms to a mechanical analogy, of course, being more fluid than solid in its nature, but as a shorthand model, these metaphors illustrate how a single change can result in different outcomes. An invasive non-native like cheatgrass alters a desert landscape quickly and irrevocably, and though that ecosystem responds with new changes of both cooperative and competitive sorts, it never returns to its original form. Likewise, water makes a desert bloom, and though its withdrawal allows aridity to return, the same ecosystem will not be back—as Heraclitus might have said, you cannot step into the same desert twice.

Some refer to the Middle East, where irrigation projects made the desert bloom many millennia ago, as the cradle of civilization, the introduction of water not only making it easier to grow cereal grains and other food but requiring a state bureaucracy to administer its distribution and adjudicate disputes. On a smaller scale, Southwest American native tribes buried terracotta pots filled with water by their plants, the moisture seeping as needed through the porous material to surrounding soil. As one of the first permutations of drip irrigation, it took a scarce resource but used a light, conservative hand in using it.

The intent to conserve water by avoiding ponding, to take the guesswork out of unneighborly irrigation, to remove the fluctuations of evaporation rates and surface loss along the delivery system, helped inspire the invention of low-flow, low-pressure drip tape. The Israeli Simcha Blass is credited with starting the first drip tape company, Netafim, in 1965, helping the nearby desert farms thrive despite the intense aridity. Through a micro-hole punched every few inches, plastic drip tape slowly emits water and when properly utilized wastes almost none. If buried below ground at root level, drip tape reaches ninety-five percent efficiency with little evaporation since the surface receives moisture last, water tending to sink rather than wick upward. But its precision has a price, its plastic composition bearing an ecological toll both in production and disposal. And it can be easily befouled, as witnessed first at the beginnings and ends of rows where tape lines lay exposed, their knotted ends leaking if insufficiently tied. At any connection, it seems, at any place two different things meet, fluctuations occur.

A walk by the ends reveals plugged lines. Is the valve at the head malfunctioning, a piece of plastic crammed in the mechanism? Or maybe a spider web (with attendant spider) created while the line was detached and the fitting open? Did perennial roots many years old strangle the tape and restrict the flow (it's rare but it happens)? Has a tractor driven over the row and compressed the soil to where the line can't expand? Have voles been at work, eating the plastic and leaving holes? Worse, is there the dreaded break in the line due to an overly vigorous, overly negligent, weeder?

An overzealous chop with a hoe or a too-deep plunge with the hori-hori (digging knife) easily damages a buried drip line, turns the gallon-an-hour drip into a gallon-a-minute stream that, depending on the cut's severity, leaves a puddle at the cut or even diverts the entire flow. During weeding and harvesting smaller irrigation problems get exposed, too, to the practiced eye—a dry spot on the row tells of a befouled microperforation that can't be fixed, a bit of sediment preventing water dispersal. It might have entered the line during installation or while patching the line, or might just have evaded the 200 micron (the width of three human hairs) filter and found its way to what wasn't quite an exit.

The same process that occurs when the Ganges and the Nile deposit silt on their respective floodplains takes place on lesser rivers and streams, so drip tape, being at the proverbial end of the ditch, inevitably faces soil particles whatever its water source. Well water tends to be cleaner than surface water that may have traveled a thousand miles, collecting stray debris along the way, but sand, silt and minerals rise from the subterranean world, as well, eager to trouble man and poke a hole in the balloon of his hubris. Just as when the germination of a profligate species' single seed is deemed an *in situ* success, a single soil particle reaching a drip tape emitter is one of many possible achievements.

Drip tape, like almost every invention designed to bypass specific problems and eliminate a set of difficulties, proves itself more susceptible to minor but debilitating incidents (like a minuscule bit of grit) than the system it usurps. An example of the give-and-take or tit-for-tat that both entropy and *allos* embody, drip tape exemplifies how shrinking the chaos present in a flood irrigating system spreads the disorder elsewhere, not just that posed by errant particles but with its production, its distribution, and its disposal. It's as if inventors, eye on the specific, reach out to pull in the general to widen the problem.

Flood irrigation, of course, also epitomizes the

exchange. As a passive method utilizing gravity, only its initial creation responsible for any large entropic debt, a single gopher hole in an irrigation ditch, particularly in an area of large fill, gives erosion its chance to redistribute the entire flow, and bad timing by users results in overflows that can destroy the entire system. Sprinkler irrigation, a more modern method, though efficient in its water dispersal, requires a great deal of materials not just to move its load but electricity to provide pressure and, these days, electronics to monitor and control the system, all with their own mounting costs to the natural flow of entropy—adding the system of maintenance (available parts, distributors and technicians) gives a more honest appraisal of its debt to nature. Nature itself, even without man's intrusion, has a specific entropic loss, though one minor compared to any trickery seeking to bypass it, and "improving" it in one place inevitably degrades it elsewhere.

The word "stymie" originates from the Scottish for "one who does not see well", evolved to describe a golf moment where one player's ball obstructs another's line of play. From there, the meaning expanded to mean any obstacle—i.e., nature to large-scale farmers, or nature's pesky subset entropy, to smallholders, at least those who, despite revering nature, are unwilling to fully concede to it. There's no way around it, entropy's a stymying force that gets in one's line of play.

Technology's history shows an increasing ability to hide entropy even while increasing it. Philip Slater, in his book *The Pursuit of Loneliness*, used the phrase "the toilet assumption" to describe how we act as if we can be rid of something unwanted (like entropy) if we just flush it away, remove it from sight. Rivers long served as receptacles of our toilet assumption, factories built close by to easily dispose of waste. Meat packing plants lined banks, their scraps and blood fed to rivers and unintentionally improving local sport fishing. Sewers inevitably end there, though nowadays their contents get filtered far more thoroughly than they once did. Upstream was always the place to be, downstream not so much.

Air operates much the same as water. Just rake your fall leaves to the downstream side of your property and, barring precipitation that mats them in place, they'll blow onto the neighbor's. Unfortunately, your upwind neighbor's leaves act identically. Unless your and your neighbors' habits differ, it's a wash. Wind and water streams both carry loads, swift ones lifting more than slower counterparts but all losing portions of their cargo when stymied by obstacles—rocks, trees, and other objects. Gold panners look for such places in waterways, since heavy gold particles are first to drop, finding them behind rocks or other changes in streams. Seed collectors might take that cue were their airborne load as valuable as gold.

When your neighbor fails to control his thistle patch you'll know—by the thistles germinating on your property in the coming years—the local wind patterns. You'll easily determine where the lee side is and how far it extends. In the winter, snow patterns reveal the same process, drifts forming on the downwind side of fences and perennials left in the field. Even a dirt clod can start what scientists call an *autocatalytic* system, one that self-generates—a dune or a drift gets bigger with each bit blown in, as it forms becoming more of an obstacle that forces more snow or sand to collect. Just for giggles, though, nature changes up the prevailing wind directions now and then so seeds, snow and silt can arrive from other directions.

Soil moves downstream in its way, too, courtesy of gravity. If you build a wall or a terrace, you experience mass-wasting when the soil behind your once-upright wall first forces it atilt, then pushes it over. Speed up that slow exertion of gravity and you witness a stream flow, and though a mound of soil doesn't seek a flat level as water does, it does stop slipping downstream when it strikes its "angle of repose", a point where the pebbles quit rolling and the particles stop sifting downward.

You might use any of these—water, wind, soil—and the process that moves them as a metaphor for ideas, for memory, for the self itself, since those all move downstream, too, sometimes taking circuitous, tumultuous paths backwards but never fully making it upstream like a salmon does. The Buddhists' *vijnana* emphasizes the flowing, downstream nature of the self, never quite a separate thing and never quite that same, separate thing it once was. When you spend time choosing, regretting, reminiscing, you create your own eroding process, a cyclical eddying force that makes minor increments of progress upstream, then pulls downstream, taken by a greater and encompassing law. You might even call the self an autocatalytic system, since the more time you spend with it the more massive it gets.

"He could make water flow upstream" farmers joke, the phrase sometimes referring to someone lucky or skilled but at other times, accompanied by an ironic wink, to someone a bit too self-important. Time, like water, doesn't flow upstream. Some theorists claim their equations suggest otherwise, that time can move the other way, just doesn't, but our intuition can't see a broken teacup reassembling itself. The most dogged of us, even without the physicist's equations, still try to do just that, though, to undo what's been done, fix what's been ruined, wanting to believe that everything has its "born again" component. And we refuse to accept evidence to the contrary.

The biologist C.H. Waddington coined the term *chreode* to describe the pathway of a cell from its open-routed inception to its "decision" to form part of a specialized organ, and other fields of study coopted the notion of a "necessary route" (chreode's Greek root meaning) to describe how rainfall at a watershed's peaks trickled downstream, its flow foreseeable via probable routes but often detoured in other directions, perhaps never actually reaching the rivulet, the brook, the river it most likely should find. Decision makers can benefit from using the chreode model, particularly if they remember that time and water flow downstream, despite their theoretical alternative.

Those subject to "failure to launch" already use the model, albeit unconsciously, when they take no path at all rather than limiting their possible futures by choosing one chreode over another. To pick possible spouse "A" or job "C" means ending all the other routes to other, perhaps better, spouses or jobs. In an occupation like farming, keeping all options open sometimes proves to be the smart choice, but also may just mean being indecisive. Since chreodes don't remain open paths forever, the impetus of time, perhaps unbeknownst to you, moves you past alternatives whether you take a specific path or no path at all.

When you pinch an annual cut flower to produce more blooms, when you prune a woody to create longer stems, you physically illustrate chreodes. The single stem you cut, even as it heals from the amputation, immediately forms new paths in the form of multiple stems that branch below the violence, reversing the pulling force of gravity that moves rainfall through pathways to the ocean. That gravity is mirrored by the sun's rays' pull, urging the species skyward, and also in the plant's genetic impetus to grow. But there are limits to the lengths of the paths engendered. Cut a mature lilac's spent blooms just a foot deep and next year's new shoots will only be roughly a foot long, perhaps shorter. Cut them six feet deep, and the new stems might recoup those six feet the next year. They, like you, reach a place of maturity at which they grow no larger, confined by their genetic limitations to a maximum size.

Some flower species have a single chreode that pinching just eliminates without inspiring alternative paths—lilies, tulips, and many other bulb crops among them. If you cut a dormant tulip bulb in half you reveal what would have been its only possible future, all its parts there in miniature—perhaps the source of the medieval notion that an adult person grew from an identical, minute form already present in the sperm cell, with that *simulacrum* in turn coming from an even smaller replica of itself, ad infinitum. Tulip bulb growers sample their harvests, often with x-ray equipment, to determine whether bulbs possess a flower or are "choked", having only a stem.

Orlaya, many rudbeckias, the Queen Anne's Lace cultivar "Green Mist", send out initial blooms from the center and then secondary efforts in a circle around it that bloom a few days later. That first bloom tends to come on a thick stem often too bulky for easy use, needs to be trimmed of sideshoots, but the ring of blooms surrounding it that open later (and on shorter stems) make harvest easy. Pinching this central bloom early saves work later on in the season. Once it's removed, many blooms, often coming at an identical time, become harvestable with little wasted effort, cut as if they were multiple hands of a clock and chiming simultaneously.

Sometimes farmers pinch side shoots rather than the central bloom, to funnel energy away from diversions and make the single flower larger. Peony growers strip side buds early in the season to increase the primary bloom's size. Your parents no doubt tried a similar tactic when they steered you (without success) from routes they deemed unprofitable.

Damming rivers to divert their flow amounts to pinching them, forcing water into chreodes otherwise not likely taken. The single stem flow becomes multi-stemmed, blooming across what typically would be desert. Historians attribute desert irrigation systems with the origin of culture and state, since managing those many stems and their resultant disputes requires a vast bureaucracy.

John Wesley Powell, an early explorer to the West, returned from his expedition to suggest lands be surveyed in such a way as to democratize water use, so that distant grazers, for instance, might still have access to a stream for drinking water. But powers-that-be instead directed the grid system, which we still employ, to be used. As a consequence, those with land by waterways controlled them, became the "Mormons upstream" that their figuratively downstream counterparts cursed. Sometimes those early land grabbers wound up being on the end of the proverbial ditch, though, when reservoirs installed later drowned their properties to further change the chreode distribution. Those inclined to foster schadenfreude might call that event an illustration of karma.

Every action, so looked at, sits in a web, one not stationary but moving like a flock. Water, air, soil and even time flow in a stream, we as conscious entities discovering our pathways, the more fortunate of us upstream, the less so at the end of the row.

———

Companion planting is an ancient effort, one periodically resurrected, to recreate or match that Edenic flow of nature where everything works, everything fits. It's an Ikea-style embracement of Zen, an inauthentic reproduction of Taoist thought, if inadvertently so. Situate X near susceptible plants to ward off particular pests; put A by B since they grow better when planted together. Apply all the proper techniques, make all the necessary connections, and nature assents to your will, provides you exactly what you want. As a paean to Eastern ideas or the Pythagorean notion that the universe has a mathematical, tight structure it succeeds, and as a subset of a broader idea, diversity, it bears some legitimacy—monocropping does indeed attract diseases and pests more readily and with more devastating effects than do small plots of interspersed species. But for an idea that purports to follow closely nature's movement, when fleshed out it becomes extremely linear, a building block model that can't possibly replicate nature's fluidity or propensity for change.

Just as eyeing the Empire State Building or Butte, Montana's Madonna fixes a pedestrian or driver's attention, a single large plot of unbroken color and texture likely draws an insect's focus—that's just math. And a well-loved plant source with a plethora of cloned neighbors makes it simple for infestations to multiply, whereas interspersing less tasty species around favored ones impedes progress. That's just math, too. But no mystical essence attaches to the process, no magical quality that acts like hidden magnets, opposite polarities attracting and like ones repelling, exists.

Appropriate as the impulse to a broad, unified view may be, companion planting and its close cousin, the astrological planting and harvesting guide, exemplify a linear understanding of the world. It starts with a picture of nature in motion—so far, so good—but it's a sealed picture, finite and machinelike and as if in a snow globe, within its boundaries a series of equations available for the farmer, all of them advising to do this to get that. It harkens back to numerology and alchemy, talismanic enterprises aiming to get from one point to another via a lost, arcane knowledge that unlocks the universe—closed views prone to the manipulative viewpoint, that of the outside observer or experimenter working on his private project. The Christian eschatological outlook, where God's final judgment ends history, and the Aristotelian notion of *telos*, an inherent purpose drawing us toward it, both echo companion planting's linearity, a tidy solution so tempting that it arises every few decades—and stays until those who embrace it pay enough attention to see it doesn't work.

Integrated Pest Management, a more scientific AND holistic approach to dealing with agricultural difficulties that substitutes logic for wishful thinking, relies on calibration and so responds to a changing universe. IPM practitioners know predator and prey species and the relationships between them, but they know, too, that variables constantly shift, hence they watch for population movements and adjust their tinkering accordingly. Their work never ends, they know no permanent solution exists, particularly since the predator population, once it's done its job, still requires a food source which managers must nurture. Almost paradoxically, that food source is the very pest they seek to control. The true heroes of the movement to shrink chemical disruption of the ecosystem, IPMers juggle species and population numbers as dramatically as Chinese acrobats manipulate, from atop a bicycle, plates spinning on lengthy sticks.

In a greenhouse, juggling a few species' populations, though difficult, is doable. Dump in some ladybugs, distribute a few spores of *Nosema locustae* (a pathogen to control grasshoppers), add lacewings, irrigate in the nematode *Heterohabditis bacteriophora* for root weevil, maybe spray on a little *Bacillus thuringiensis*, watch for aphids, investigate for spider mites, for leaf miners, grow a few tasty plants for the pests to work on and multiply just enough to feed predators through slack time. Two thousand square feet, some intense focus through it on a slow walk with piercing attention, squat where you see something odd, scrape the ground, look at stems, under leaves. Look for differences and when you see them, investigate. It's a sort of poetry, a wielding of balance and symmetry within a confined medium, but take the walls away from that particular piece of greenhouse property and it transforms from a haiku-like confined entirety to a subset of a Tolstoyan larger whole—it becomes *allos*.

Whether the size of a greenhouse or multiple acres, the farmer cultivates only the cusps of any whole, a small percentage of land where his practices and the insect populations they succor or hinder differ from those of the surrounding, much larger areas. Hence, no matter his talents or lack thereof, the propensities lurking nearby rush in—the hundred thousand grasshopper-infested acres adjacent ignore his efforts, the tarnished plant bugs in the alfalfa of abutting pivot systems move in when hay gets swathed, the aphids sweeping through the thousands of nearby acres of wheat stop by for a different snack. So long as no major perturbations transpire in the ecosystem enveloping his, he might fiddle with his insect, fungus and bacteria-balancing act with some success. If he's a true believer he'll attribute favorable outcomes to his appropriate actions, unfavorable ones to inappropriate manipulations: too little of this, too much of that, applied in the wrong way at the wrong time. He won't however, consider his beliefs to be falsely premised.

Believing is like being in a greenhouse, the belief system the plastic separating a small portion of the world from its remaining, greater portion. Sufficiently involved in your activity, it's easy to forget that clear plastic lining, easy to be settled into those grid cells of your brain that identify only this portion of space and its contents and ignore all else. If you believe in truth, however, that greenhouse gets a lot bigger—when you hit your head against one plastic wall you realize the world's a much larger place, and when you hit your head against a second one you know that it's much bigger yet.

Remember the Serenity Prayer? How it separates what's in your field of operation and what lies outside it? Well, a more structured and precise model of that idea preceded it by some forty years as Bertrand Russell's Theory of Logical Types. It noted how most misunderstanding comes from miscategorizing one level of speech as another, collapsing a hierarchy that if understood could settle most ignorance. Thus, a class of chairs is itself not a chair, and the class of classes of chairs is not a class (Bateson called this a meta-class to further ease discussion). Think of a greenhouse, then that greenhouse, along with three others, under a larger greenhouse (a meta-greenhouse), then that meta-greenhouse with three more just like it under a meta-meta-greenhouse. Seems complicated, right? It can be, and as a tool needn't be used until that moment it is required to sort out the tangled mass of human communication. And belief.

Most believers primarily practice deduction to ferret out understanding, starting out with accepted premises and fitting facts, of whatever size and shape, into stories that fulfill those foundations. *All swans are white*, they might assert, and if a black bird shows up that sounds like a swan, looks like a swan, and will even mate with a swan they just deny it's a swan. You can always make up a story to fit your beliefs. If someone tells you that a spray of milk and baking soda on your plants makes them grow better, when you use that method it will seem to work whether it does or not.

Karl Popper helped sort out this problem somewhat with his Falsification Principle, claiming that if a premise isn't testable and falsifiable it sits outside scientific or logical study—though it might be true, it can't be proven so (because you won't admit a black swan disproves your white swan theory) and is thus a waste of the scientist's time and effort. Many "natural" methods fall into the unfalsifiable category, stemming from an urge to believe nature simple and controllable and adjusting one's perception of results in order to keep that greenhouse film above intact. Thus it "seems" a method controls aphids, but without a controlled area where the method wasn't used there's no way to falsify it. It "seems" like there were fewer grasshoppers after bait was applied, but were hopper populations down elsewhere, too? It's a typical human failing to desire order and to keep information that confirms one beliefs and discard anomalies that refute them.

Companion planting fits that pattern. It presumes balance. Ignores competition as it emphasizes cooperation. In so doing, it collapses logical levels into a seamless singularity, for balance in the greenhouse isn't balance in the meta-greenhouse isn't balance in the meta-meta-house. And cooperation in the greenhouse isn't cooperation in the meta-greenhouse, and so on. Each semi-contained ecosystem has its ranges, parameters, and biases that fall by the wayside when seen against a larger context, so only in a tightly enclosed space, perhaps a terrarium, perhaps a greenhouse, does the notion of balance work.

———

How is a farmer like a jet plane? They both whine on the way to Hawaii. The joke makes the rounds in both the United States and Europe, farmers having a universal reputation as unjustified complainers.

Poor me, poor me. Weather. Prices. The government. Those are just the big gripes. Smaller ones: the help, engineers with ideas that end up badly in the field; suppliers; clients; the neighbors. No wonder mankind came up with those momentary breaks in the day— prayer—and the Sabbath day off, the world needed a respite of giving thanks to balance out the grousing.

In some sense, the complaints replace "knocking on wood" as a way to ward off ominous events. Maybe farmers aren't really unhappy, just want to make sure there's a fenceline between the outside and the precious inside. It's a bit of a pretense, their version of Brahman's casting out Maya to hide himself from himself, a diversionary tactic not so much to express untruth as for a little bit of playfulness. It's a way to cover one's tracks.

Optimism provides the same function, a perimeter equivalent to a set of hex signs to ward off evil. Look at the bright side. Everything happens for a reason.

You're lucky it wasn't worse. It all works out in the end. Neither grievance nor applause, though, provides much of a deterrent to outsiders, no more than does planting euphorbia on the property line to deter gophers. Maybe they don't like euphorbia, but gophers can walk above ground and start tunneling on the other side. Here's another one: use a bed of daffodils to deter deer. True, deer don't eat daffodils, but they can prance across a pretty big field of them to get to what's tasty beyond.

The fencelines we erect come almost instinctively, and then we add finishing touches to our genetics' original intent. But as *allos* would predict, few fences lack a gate or two, just as no moat lacks a bridge, and many living things possess the equivalent of gates as stomata— openings that allow inside out and outside in. Plant leaves breathe through pores, which close in hot weather in order to lower transpiration rates, and humans expel oil and sweat through theirs. The Pollyannaish optimist and the gruff pessimist alike figuratively sweat a lot, their breathing rates dependent on how effectively their perimeters operate.

What goes in, what goes out. Scientists separate sensations somewhat along those lines into categories of *reafferent* and *exafferent*, the latter experienced as outside information coming in by sentient creatures as simple as the amoeba, the former type resulting from actively retrieving information—a hand going out into a bucket of Legos, an eye scanning the horizon, a sniff test of a bouquet. The borders we create filter exafferent information, can ease that overwhelming burden of information coming in, but also sift (sometimes unwittingly) our efforts going out into the world.

Freud presented a roughly equivalent typology, the neurotic expecting the world to come to him (the exafferent fun-sucker) and the psychotic imposing himself upon the world (the reafferent blustery alcoholic). Were we to similarly saw the agricultural world into two pieces we'd see the commercial, psychotic farmer on one side of our cut and the neurotic no-tiller on the other, the least psychotic meeting the least neurotic at the abyss positioned mid-spectrum.

The whine and complaint act much like the skunk's scent glands, like the thistle's spiny leaves, like the rose's thorny stem. Like those natural protective devices, which keep at least some enemies at a distance, it ends up as a tool of collateral serendipity: strangely shaped seeds parachuting on the wind snag on thorns and spines to find their *in situ* positions—examples of true, if ironic, companion planting—and those unafraid of gruff exteriors cling to the curmudgeonly. Closed to one sector of the universe, the complainer opens the gate for another, *allos* casting out a bit of its irony.

The curmudgeon stakes a position as the utopian does not, providing a sort of *axis mundi* (center of the world) for some and a landmark for others. You know where the pessimist stands, while the optimist recedes as you near him, a horizon never to be reached, never to be known. His territory staked rightly or wrongly, the pessimist gives stability to the world that the optimist never can. He has a position, one that may border yours, but doesn't envelop you as the optimist's stance does. It's often said that good fences make good neighbors, and the grumpy pessimist provides that well-identified border in a way the smiling optimist, ever-mending the disconnections between his outlook and reality, does not.

Radio hosts fear silence, the dead space that above all else loses listeners. It draws attention to itself, is a failing akin to a magician revealing the methods behind his tricks. Empty moments frighten some comedians and musicians, too, but others learn to fashion such space to their benefit. The drawn out pause or stuttering cadence, properly utilized, brings art to what might otherwise be bland sustenance. Zen visual artists use emptiness to bring prominence to a figure in a painting—open space lets attention relax, makes it easier to focus.

Flower farmers face a similar relationship to gaps in time, their conversation with their crops and land often one-sided and laden with long periods of unconsummated expectations. Start with winter for those in climes with seasons, a desired rest after a hard frost on one end and an antsy anticipation as snow melts on the other, midway through hope ballooning if memories of toil have withered. Planners get lost in their private metaverse during this crop silence, toy with spreadsheets like pre-teen boys reading box scores and sorting baseball cards. Mythmaking percolates, its aesthetic daydreams sifting through past detritus to create impossible futures. And then, the punchline called spring...

To be successful you have to know your audience (comedians say "READ THE ROOM!"), so those farmers in climates with long, gentle springs cast a different routine upon their acreage than those with a more boisterous, demanding crowd where winter turns immediately to summer, only a couple days called spring to separate them—little more than a bathroom break, really. For the no-spring farmers, the lackadaisical winter pace they cultivated proves suddenly inadequate, tasks now peppering them like rowdy hecklers soon to turn the crowd to mob. Squelch the loudest first, put it in its place and expect its return. Be ruthless if you must, it attacked first.

Before they go onstage comedians have a joke list, musicians have a set list, and farmers have a sequence of tasks similar to a MASH unit's triage policy: the medic's hierarchy of emergency, priority, and non-urgent becomes the farmer's what-needs-done-now, what-needs-done-soon, and what-needs–to-be-done-eventually. Just as audience laughter (or lack thereof) might force the comedian off-script, just as the bar crowd's nervous level and drunkenness might require a rearrangement of songs, the farmer's rough plan becomes mostly ad lib as he fumbles through the year's emergencies and unforeseen events.

Most humor requires a jack-in-the-box moment of surprise, perhaps explaining why flower farmers continually try new crop varieties. Every new bloom brings the same wonder to the grower that a jack-in-the-box brings to an infant, with just enough time passing from year to year to keep the joke fresh. Perennials particularly jump into consciousness as surprise, their typical bloom periods often a matter of just three weeks, at best, before they go back in the box to be forgotten. Though annuals deliver a similar jolt the first time they flower, if sequence planted they remain in bloom for months and lose, like an oft repeated joke, their power to please. There has to be a setup for a punchline, a sort of spacing that repeated blooming lacks.

Other gaps, courtesy of the weather, appear most frequently in spring, nature having left one season and heading for another but indecisive of what to wear. Hot, cold, wet, dry and windy—often in the same day. It's hard to plant or plow during bouts of heavy precipitation, unpleasant to do so in periods of strong winds, fruitless to do it when cold. "Hurry and wait", the adage goes, the farmer on call like a fireman, ready to slip on his work clothes at the first sign of bad weather abatement. Wait for the soil to dry out enough to work and plant. Wait for the iron nights, that three-day stretch of frost, to pass so transplants can be set out. Hit it hard, wait again, hit it hard and wait again.

A different sort of gap shows up in bloom times and their less attractive twin that follows them, marketing periods. An eerie silence comes after early bulb crops finish up, and though greenhouses and coolers help drag out that first flower flush beyond its natural bloom period, the sales van may empty as it waits for peonies and perennials to ramp up production. Another bloom silence appears on many farms between the "perennial glut", the period when most long-term species flower, and the onset of annual production. Again, the cooler lengthens by a few days how long the perennials can be sold, but holding time is finite before quality severely suffers. Those open spots between flowering seasons, welcome to some degree in their offering of harvesting respites, create anxiety from a sales perspective—if the farmer delivers little or nothing to his clients, won't his clients go elsewhere for their purchases? Onstage and having forgotten the song, audience awaiting and having misplaced his joke list, the farmer fumbles for any Zen aplomb he may have acquired when polishing past embarrassments. Though he aims for continuous sales flow, he knows it to be nearly impossible, know his clients' purchases fluctuate, too, due to trends, sudden events or, as frequently happens in resort towns, slack times. Lighten up, he tells himself, a few gaps in his delivery match the many gaps in theirs, no use lamenting that those gaps don't perfectly overlap.

Many species, particularly perennials, tie the arrival of their inflorescences to daylength or temperature. If that relationship is too exactly matched, the grower has few options to lengthen the bloom season—if he plants early, they just grow bigger and taller before blooming; if later, they bloom when too short. Cool weather crops especially take their cue from temperature levels, growing best when it's cool and their blooms triggered by heat, so multiple plantings, possible in places with long springs, fail where the weather skips a gear between winter and summer. A grower with gambling tendencies or an overactive confidence (are those the same thing?) may try to stagger-plant those species in his short-spring climate and on rare years of extended cool weather get a fine second, or even third, crop. It's all a matching game, joke-to-audience, song-to-listeners, species to climate-and-soil, with an omnipresent hope for plentiful harvest, but misjudging the relationship—say, by planting cool crops too late or warm weather crops too soon—ends up with the crowd leaving.

Restaurateurs, not being oracular, can't predict clientele fluctuations even when aware of holidays and local events, and flower farmers likewise can't foresee aberrations in weather or customer behavior. But a Zen farmer might hedge his prophecies by not trying to thread the needle, planting slightly too much rather than too little (best to keep the customer happy) and stretching the season where possible. He omits those species tightly embedded in time and temperature—let the tinkerers work at that problem—but takes advantage of the crops with wide windows of temperament. That catalogue makes up his joke set, his song list, and he gets better every time he performs it, every year's climate a new audience whose nuances he watches closely.

Novice and experienced farmers alike must situate themselves in their climate—*READ THE ROOM!* To be more exact, their climate already situates them but they need to be aware of how they're positioned in that particular *boid* flock, or they'll be flying into frost, drought, wind and other vagaries of the atmosphere. Many small farmers enter the profession armed with little more than a USDA hardiness zone map that shows the low temperatures typically afflicting an area. That helps direct a grower to avoid species that won't survive on their farm but climate includes much more information.

For instance, compare just three zone 5 locations to see how incomplete the USDA map is: Madison, Wisconsin has a growing season of 162 days, Logan, Utah's is 131 days, and Blackfoot, Idaho comes in at 92 days—70 days less than its Wisconsin cohort. Logan has 35 more sunny days than Madison and half the precipitation, and Blackfoot has about half of Logan's moisture total—that means tweaking irrigation, but also changes the plant list, each species being attuned to a specific amount of sun or shade. The three areas exhibit stark differences that a single map can't convey, allowing crops like Tuberose (once *Polianthes tuberosa,* now *Agave amica*) to prosper in long season Madison while they just start blooming as temperatures wane and days shorten in Blackfoot, making them failures in all but extremely warm years.

Though many growers know their last spring frost date and when their first fall frost occurs, a more accurate way to approach that statistic is to ask what your risk aversion is and then match it with the likelihood of severe temperature. There's a 10% chance in Logan that temperatures drop to 24 degrees on April 8, but in Madison the same chance still exists on May 4, in Blackfoot, May 7. If 32 degrees is your fright point, there's a ten percent chance of that in Blackfoot clear into June 15, in Logan on May 20.

Many variables, most Google-able with a little patience but some more obscure, affect any particular locality. Wind patterns, for instance. Or sudden changes in temperature—Chinooks hitting east of the Continental Divide might move the thermometer seventy degrees in twenty-four hours, a difficult change to prepare for. Humidity. Altitude. Latitude. Daylength. Number of cloudy days. Accumulated heat units. And over the long term, variability year to year—Southeast Idaho has summers when temperatures reach ninety degrees just three or four times, while other years that total soars to forty; its winters, much the same, may not rise above freezing from Halloween to March one year but on another sport a summer-like January that inspires daffodils to bloom and summons peonies from dormancy. And though its Zone 5 designation means the area might suffer twenty below nights, in the last two decades it's only happened once—while in the 1980s it was common to see ten day spells of such cold, daytime temperatures struggling to reach zero.

Snow cover, being an insulator, makes a big difference, too. A plant labeled zone 5 or 6 survives just fine in zone 3 with adequate blankets of snow, though it won't make it through droughty, open winters. When Anchorage, Alaska suffered a snowless winter, ten feet deep water pipes froze, a safe depth on normal years when several feet of snow keep the soil warm.

It takes a deft statistician to ferret out other important weather variables, like the likelihood of Indian summer (or its unnamed, but much cursed, cold twin) events that fool plants into either premature activity or sudden shutdowns from which they may never recover. Add the prevalence of freeze/thaw episodes, when surface soil saturates with snowmelt but cannot drain through the frozen soil layer beneath. In these conditions roots absorb water, swell and then freeze, the fickleness of temperatures exploding cells, cracking and rotting roots. And what is the likelihood of a plant killing temperature or a bloom destroyer throughout a given spring—while the likelihood of one frosty night in an area might be tolerable, what is the likelihood of that nasty temperature day after day, over the entire period covering bud to bloom? Does sudden cold occur more frequently or less during warm springs or cold ones—or is there a relationship at all? It only takes one hard frost to ruin spring blooms like bleeding hearts (*Dicentra*), fritillaria, hellebores or foxtail lilies (*Eremerus*), to kill forsythia buds or end a lily crop just recently emerged from the soil, so a grower needs to know if frost threatens occasionally or with regularity.

Seed sellers sometimes label their packets with the number of days from germination to bloom, but few newcomers understand that those days refer not to time but to a more complex calculation, one that accounts for units of temperature available for growth. The equation? A growing degree day equals Temperature(max) + Temperature(min)/2-T(base). Sounds complex? Compared to minutes and hours, it surely is. But once you get a generalized feel for the relationship between your climate and the "days" on the seed packet, you understand that what your extension agent calls your 120 day growing season—a very rough calculation identifying time between last frost in the spring and first frost in the fall—isn't nearly long enough for a 120 day species. Both measurements may be labeled "days", but they bear little likeness save some etymological DNA.

Plants don't grow much when temperatures exceed 86 degrees, so any hours of intense heat get thrown out of the local climate equation, and each species has a minimum temperature beneath which no growth takes place, eliminating more hours and days—springtime days, always shorter in terms of light hours even when unseasonably warm, often contribute no growing time at all in bitter spells. The equation's base temperature is where plant growth hits zero, and is a figure that differs species to species. Cereal and forage crops, for instance, develop very little below 40 degrees. Germinating warm season crops like celosia and zinnias ahead of time proves useless if you transplant them before the climate meets their base temperature.

Another variable farmers often pay little attention to: the relationship between the sun and earth. They know the sun rises in the east and sets in the west, but remain unaware how closely the sun clings to the south horizon as winter hits, how it ends up on the North side of the sky in early and mid-summer (at least in the northern hemisphere). As a consequence, the sweet peas planted in shade in April end up in full sun in July, resulting in short, unmarketable blooms, and the sun-loving sunflower seeded near a windbreak in early May's light struggle in the shade of late July, may bloom after sunflowers planted elsewhere on the acreage.

Frost pockets develop. Even a minor dike creates a haven for cold air, and hillsides notoriously feed chilliness to the vales below them. An upright freezer filled with smoke, then cooled, when opened will spill its contents as a solid rectangular block that looks much like ice, an astonishing illustration of how cold drops—a farmer needs to be aware of vulnerable areas mimicking that action. Nighttime lows might be ten degrees different in two locations just a mile apart, even in equally flat areas, depending on the locality's position in wind flows and nearness to rivers or trees. Quick changes from moments of frost to sudden intense morning sunlight might cause problems, but so can lengthy periods in the morning shade cast by a building that add up the hours of frost. Dry plants succumb to frost much sooner than recently irrigated counterparts—in large potato fields it's easy to see where wind skips occurred in a field, the under-watered crop blackened by even minimal frost and adjoining strips irrigated a day sooner unscathed. Protective coverings like walls of water might actually hold frost in at times, killing tomatoes while unprotected ones survive, but at other times do their job very well. Other coverings mustn't touch the vegetation they cover lest they counterproductively assist frost rather than prevent it.

Heavy dews combined with intense light create problems for flower farmers, their white flowered blooms browning when a wet surface magnifies morning sun. Sudden strong light, as well as hot wind, browns even yellow petaled species like heliopsis and sunflowers, and blisters late tulips, particular when dry.

A farmer, then, sits in a crosshatch of weather variables (he may feel like he's in the crosshairs) of which he must be aware but which must not obsess him. They're his audience, but they didn't necessarily come for his show— they might listen, they might not, they might heckle him, they might clap. Once he reads the room, though, scopes out their nature and position, imagining them perhaps as *boids*, he can settle into his movements, acquaint himself with both boisterousness and silence, correcting minor mistakes he makes as he, as well as the objects and currents around him, continue to shift.

Zen attends to the everyday, which the event-centeredness of the flower business in many ways contradicts. Most flower sales wrap around holidays, funerals, weddings, important moments—70 percent to Christmas, Hannukah, Valentine's Day, Easter, and

Mother's Day, 20 percent for weddings and funerals—while the work of the farmer is more the long slog, the everyday tasks of nurturing and harvesting plants. Most anyone who has worked a Valentine's holiday will admit that "feeling the love" goes by the wayside days before the actual holiday, as long hours, accumulated mishaps and cranky customers drain all goodwill away. And funerals? Any bucket route driver has seen designers poring over the obituary page, less intrigued by grief than an increase in clientage.

Flower farming is a paradox in many ways: the sale of the fresh and perishable but touting vase longevity; the—to some—tedious everyday experience of growing and then the momentary explosive display at an event; the inartistic wrestling with mud and dust, insect and fungus and weather, and then the clean, aesthetically pleasing design work that strips away distastefulness. As one moves down the production line, from farming to display, Zen becomes increasingly difficult to embody, the shrillness of being event-centered akin sometimes to a howling arctic wind—just ask any wedding planner about "Bridezilla" or her stepmother.

Early Protestants ridiculed Catholic monks, claiming it was easy enough to be saintly in the protected confines of a monastery, much harder out in a world filled with sinners and temptation. The same might be said about Zen flower farmers: in the silence (or loneliness) of a flower field, amid the textures and colors of nature, buried in physical tasks that peg the mind and body to a particular time and place, being Zen is "easy", but put them in the design room as the wedding or event nears and see how Zen they are.

Every milieu has its pace, its objects, their size, velocity and direction that the brain configures and the mind then typically confounds. Those configurations change, the border, grid and place cells rearranging as quickly as possible, but the mind is far slower to react, having cast its own blankets of concepts and emotions (the meta) upon the map. The more no-mind you possess, then, the more likely you slip from one arena to another, from the farm to the sales route to the meetings with the event planner, but most of us are more like the monk, enlightened at the monastery but panicky at the airport.

One face when working with a funerary entourage, another for a young bride-to-be, a certain presence when employees as a group are around, a different one for each employee during one-on-ones, yet another for the delivery driver, an appropriate voice for collection but altered when taking orders, still another when fielding complaints. But then the favorite one, the face of being alone with the plants, hands in the soil, sun upon you—a monkish face, no doubt, a no-face that doesn't register in your attention. To move seamlessly with that face between areas, to absorb interruption without becoming angry or being stricken dumb, and to be authentic doing so—now that would be a feat. No question, to do all that would be Zenlike, but who, without practice, might be that person?

Some comedians use an audience's nervousness to their advantage, knowing the possibility of being singled out, ridiculed or made the center of attention, keeps members perched deeply in the present. The farmer sits equally alert, the quality of his alertness giving away his Zen-ness: if he is ready to stumble without worry of embarrassment when the next shift of duties comes, if he meets it not as disruption but as a surprise akin to comic relief, let's call him Zen.

Liebig's Law of the Minimum, a staple of soil science, states "if one of the essential plant nutrients is deficient, plant growth will be poor even when all the other essential nutrients are abundant." The law might justly be applied to any business, and on a flower farm it equates to a sad fact for some: their weakness, not their strength, will dictate their success. A talented grower that markets poorly: failure. An excellent marketer without agricultural skills: failure. Someone great with the books but can't deal with customers: failure. An area of high proficiency doesn't cover for disability in another.

Taking the Zen attitude with you through the entire farm-to-event process might be difficult, the equivalent of posing as the eye amidst a hurricane, but not doing so doesn't erase Zen-ness from possibility. If your endeavor succeeds by your standards, if you know your weakness and know how it hampers success but find satisfaction, even humor, in the structure and outcome of what you do, you may indeed still be Zen, your imperfection a finishing touch, homage to nature.

———

Inside either the Buddhist no-self or the no-till/ organic discourse, the respective debate seems logical, but viewed from the outside the fineness of the arguments appears trivial, as laughable as playground football played by the less-than-athletic to coaches looking on— the bickering over each play (You were out of bounds! Was not!) (That was a fumble! No it wasn't!), the small increments of social climbing that show themselves, all belying the event's importance. Inside the occasion of the game, the players bury themselves seriously into every action, while on the hillside, sandwiches in hand, the coaches observe with hilarity. A player looking up to see himself through the coaches' eyes may walk away forever from an enterprise he fully enjoyed but no longer can.

Such embarrassment trails us instant to instant, self to self, sometimes all our lives. Aptly born from *baraca*, a Portuguese word for "noose", embarrassment ties the present to the past and strangles us. To be fair, though, so does regret. And nostalgia. And for that matter, pride—embarrassment's fuel. Maybe, upon close perusal, remembering is the noose, embarrassment just one way to knot it.

At the end of every row, at the juncture of each occasion, lies a snare set with such a noose, ready not just for those looking back but for those peering ahead, those full of worry, those riddled with apprehension, those excitedly anticipating. A farmer attending to his task, refusing the trap's enticing bait, steps right over it. But looking either back or ahead more than briefly, he gets snared. For every three ensnared animals another chews off a limb to escape—caught in our embarrassments or discovered while foolishly daydreaming we would do the same were we brave enough. Were we Zen we wouldn't get caught, of course, but when snared and wanting to be Zen, well, we need to do some figurative chewing, imbed ourselves in the present.

A plan can be a trap. Its elegance, its thoroughness, its historical tie to its maker, beg to be adhered to—in the stream we call *vijnana* it's the equivalent of an old car body placed to shelter trout and foster water fauna, a surface for aquatic flora to collect upon and adhere to, a spot for differences to erupt and change to emerge. It can be so enchanting you may never leave it even when you need to.

Even if you say you have no plan, you likely have one. A rudimentary one, maybe, hidden like *hintergedanken* not far removed from Kant's innate structures of space and time. A plan not beset with excess detail or tiny, incremental steps, but one that situates you in the present with a good, if vague, understanding of where you've been and where you're going, in a sort of *betweenness* we refer to as "now" and "here". Such a simulation cast into the future, applied lightly like a scuffle hoe, assists movement through the world. Too much recollection or imagination, however, stymies the present and stalls the future; it's a problem faced by the autistic who remember too well, the structures that in a normal brain swell with short-term information, that then shrink away into generalizations, instead solidifying in theirs—a typical brain remembers a forest, an autistic one remembers every tree. A plan can be just such a hindrance when every detail has equal and imminent importance.

Too many ideas, too many tools, too many details of any kind—like those in an overly conceived plan—create a kind of clutter that impedes moving through any milieu. The order sought when collecting and building those things results instead in disorder, an over-detailed existence seen in the houses of hoarders, where traipsing from one space to another resembles a rush-hour crawl through traffic. True, you can sense position only by understanding the world and yourself, creating some sort of meta-world to reference the actual, but you do so more efficiently and effortlessly when unburdened by excessive knowledge. Reynolds' *boids,* when programmed with extra instructions that were more precise in detail, ended up crashing into obstacles and each other. If you've negotiated through some governmental regulations you know the feeling, will immediately understand that too many rules impede, rather than aid, movement—as much so as no rules at all.

Zeno's Paradox might be applied to the end of the row. A layman, being pragmatic, might consider Zeno's thought experiment a foolish waste of time, but philosophers still toy with it two plus millennia later—it's a favorite snare for them. It states that an object, perhaps an arrow, can never get to its target with the instructions to "go half the way there" at step one, then at step two go half the distance remaining, then half of that, and so forth. The halves get smaller but the arrow never reaches the end. A recalcitrant weeder tackling a row might pep talk himself into a better attitude by similarly halving the task, that imaginary shrinkage somehow lessening the task's oppressiveness. When he gets to the halfway point he looks at what remains, does half of that, and continues on, but unlike Zeno, when he gets close to the end he just finishes. If as a young child you swept a floor with a broom and dustpan you likely came up with this argument without giving it a philosophical overtone: you can never pick up that last little bit of dust, so you just hide it the best you can.

Though Zeno wouldn't have admitted it, that last dust may be the most essential part of his paradox, the *allos* that evades a perfectly closed system. No farmer would intentionally stand at the end of the row splitting halves into halves, would instead either leave his project as "good enough" or finish it, but his broader work demands do have the character of never being done. There's always just one more thing to do.

It feels a bit like that child's game, Johnny setting his palm on the table, Sally putting her palm on the back of his hand, he then placing his second palm on her hand, she setting her other palm on the pile. Then Johnny pulls his hand from beneath the pile to place on top and she follows suit, on and on and on until they stop, either bored or laughing. The game, silly as it may be, might seem a child's primer to the nature of life, an early representation of the universe's hidden structures, those ruling the compost heap as well as the Buddhist *samsara*, the birth-and-death of things. Taking a step back to an adult's perspective, the game might be disturbing if certainty is your need, but conversely it can be viewed as a source of wonder, its repetition not a chain that confines but one that wanders into infinity one link at a time.

You might accuse an alcoholic of committing to a similar process, always having "just one more drink", though his activity tends to send him into a confining, repetitive cycle that gets smaller and smaller—a good example of how heading out into the open can instead send you right down into the heart of a relentless eddy. In a more self-serious arena, physicists practice a similar repetitiveness in their slicing and dicing, finding first the "smallest bit of matter", the atom, then the "smallest bits" that comprised it—neutron, proton, electron—then ever smaller bits as technology widened its abilities to discover minuteness. Stay tuned, there will be more, smaller particles yet.

The repetitive, searching activity is part curiosity, part a need for movement, and part a reafferent willfulness, applying one's sensory apparatus into the world to gather information, first toward where it yields easily, then against its walls, then beyond that layer to the next one. Sometimes it's a need to control, sometimes it's a need to connect, an attempt to extend the traditional closed-system mind to a more open and inclusive Batesonian mind, become the equivalent of *boid*-flock-atmosphere, become a part of the outside but also making the outside part of you.

One way to satisfy this reafferent urge comes via naming, a very old pastime most evident in the Bible's Genesis—in which Adam names the beasts, the birds and the fish. It's a way to triangulate—since I can't truly do a Vulcan mind meld with you, I do the next best thing by pointing to third things, naming them, describing them, in the sharing of details creating a bond of sorts, a flock of two if it's just you and me, a larger flock of it's a classroom, a larger one if it's a viewership or readership.

The naming tendency rears its head in Buddhist identification of the mind's and self's parts, the more elusive a thing we sense the more needful we are to name it. It shows up, too, in no-till's nit-picking of the best method to not-do something, in the native plant advocate's freezing a specific section of time to decide what is kosher and what isn't (and finding the same pitfalls as the authentic foodie: post-Columbian or pre-Columbian, pre- or post-Silk Road?), in the one-upmanship of any art or discipline, and in botanical taxonomy, where *Matricaria* (feverfew) was once *Tanacetum* was once *Chrysanthemum parthenium*, where *Triteleia* (cluster-lily) was (or still is?) *Brodiaea*, where other confusions exist—particularly where differences prove slight. The camp behind one name wars with the competing name's supporters—"never has so little been fought for so hard," it's been said of academic infighting. Religious hair-splitting, too, runs along similar petty lines (take a look at a rabbinical library or medieval Catholic discourse), as do the subjects of philosophical and psychological disciplines. It's our fondest urge, one might say, to stick our heads in the noose. Artist, cook, snobby wine connoisseur, we try to find the line, look beneath the surface, get beyond the horizon, push the limits, but never really get to the bottom of things—for there is no bottom. Zeno's Paradox begins to seem not like a paradox but an illustration of how life is.

Lao-Tsu, writing on this insufficiency of words and concepts, wrote, "The Tao that can be spoken of is not the Tao." The map is not the territory. The name is not the thing. Though philosophers secretly acknowledge Lao-Tsu's appraisal, they too find the scramble to identify and name too pleasurable to deny—they welcome the noose.

At the end of the row, then, Zen or not-Zen, finishing up or just getting started, looking behind or peering ahead, seeking the noose or ignoring it, proud of what you did or regretting it, even embarrassed, perhaps—go ahead and stumble, but let the self looking at the self laugh rather than experience shame—it's just the meta-world referring to the actual world, one akin to recreational tilling, with only the most diligent or saintly spared from the activity. The rest of us, including the farmer, as a flock of semi-failures, can't resist a role in the universal juggling act (*juggling,* unsurprisingly, having the same etymological source as *joking*), it being a way to churn existence, to topple the everyday routine if but for a moment. It's a way of interacting with the world, then interacting with those interactions—the ratios, the symmetries, the spacing and velocities of physical objects but also the words and concepts that refer to them—that may define what most of us think it is to be human, though the relationships between things for the normal experiencer is far different than those for the Zen acolyte. Those differences, interesting as they are to those of us infatuated with that particular noose, may not bear wasting time upon beyond an initial acknowledgment. Dwelling upon them, trying to discern an exactitude that can hardly exist in a fluid medium, starts an activity akin to that of a centrifuge. Or would that be a child's merry-go-round? Around and around and around and around...

A Buddhist parable has the Buddha sitting before a group of adherents, silently holding a blossom as each explains what it symbolizes and how it fits into Buddhist teaching. The last follower just smiles and laughs, after which the Buddha speaks. "What can be said I have said to you, and what cannot be said, I give to you," he says, handing the lotus to his successor. Apt, it being a flower and not a useful tool, not an edible food, in the Buddha's hand—let the flower farmer contemplate that.

And then forget it.

ACKNOWLEDGMENTS

FOR A WELL-WRITTEN BOOK ON navigation and recent neurological discoveries regarding our place, grid and border cells, read Michael Bond's *From Here to There: The Art and Science of Finding and Losing Our Way.* The most accessible book on Buddhism is *Christmas Humphreys' Buddhism: An Introduction and Guide.* Gregory Bateson's work includes *Mind and Nature, Angel's Fear* (written posthumously with his daughter Mary Catherine and the most readable), and *Steps to an Ecology of Mind.* For more on *boids* and the complexity science behind them, go to *Complexity: The Emerging Science at the Edge of Order and Chaos.* And while you're at it, re-read all those fables you learned as a child, they have more wisdom for you as an adult than they gave you as a child.

Printed in the United States
by Baker & Taylor Publisher Services